Health Home and Happiness

Afternoon Freezer Cooking Cookbook

Stock your freezer with grain-free favorites without spending all day in the kitchen

Table of Contents

How to Use This Book

Different family sizes, needs, and situations will use this course differently. Here we'll go over different ways to use this course so that it is the most helpful in your busy lifestyle.

1. Do a bulk cooking day when you need it

When people think of bulk cooking, they usually think of taking the entire weekend, or a full day, to put together dinners for the month. The trouble with this method is that we often do not have an entire weekend to devote just to the kitchen, and the meals can be time consuming and less health-promoting than what we would like.

When we focus on the protein and vegetables during our bulk cooking day, and then cut up some fruit and make some pre-made grain-free baked goods if we have time, everything that is now *easy* and *fast* in the fridge is also healthy!

This helps keep us on track. If we are running behind, we at least have the nutrient dense portion of our meal already done. Add an apple for a carb, and off you go!

Tips for this method:

- **Not everything can be frozen** (mayonnaise-based egg or chicken salad needs to be kept in the fridge) so pay attention to storage notes. In general, everything except ferments should be stored in the freezer if being kept longer than 1 week before use.
- **Identify your trouble meals:** For me, having Wed/Thurs/Friday breakfasts prepared for the kids, and something easy to pull out on evenings we have sports practice or plans with friends helps make the week run smoothly. Knowing that there are 3-4 meals in the freezer waiting when we get back from a weekend away or vacation makes the unpacking/catching up on laundry process work so much better.

2. Singles & Couples

If you're not feeding a family, obviously this much food will go further. You may be able to do one cooking day and then freeze half; using half this week, and half the next.

Other considerations that adults might want to take with this course:

- Intermittent Fasting is a growing tend for adults - that means that you eat during an 8 or 6-hour time block and fast from, say, 7 pm to 11 am. In this case you wouldn't need most of the breakfasts. I personally do this most of the time, but I make the breakfast items for my children.
- Adults that do eat breakfast may eat something lighter than growing children- such as a piece of fruit and couple pieces of baked bacon.
- If you're using less of the breakfasts, but still enjoy breakfast foods (who doesn't?!) just use them as your lunches and dinners. Delicious!

3. Extra Carbs & Calories

On the other end of the spectrum from what we covered in #2, is the adults, or children or teens, that need extra calories beyond what is provided in the basic cooking day.

For these people, either doubling up on the proteins, vegetables and fruit can be an option if you're staying on a specific diet like GAPS (Gut and Psychology Syndrome). But this can be costly for people who do not require being on a specific diet. For that reason, we have optional carbs that include gluten-free options like baked goods, rice, sweet potatoes, regular potatoes, and corn tortillas.

People who may benefit from these adaptations:

- Athletes
- Breastfeeding or pregnant mothers
- Teens or children in a growth spurt
- Children in general (they grow so fast!)
- Adults with physical jobs like construction

Sharing the work

If you have children, putting them to work is a great way to keep them occupied while you are cooking.

Depending on age, some good things for children to do:

- Bring in and put away groceries
- Wash fruit and vegetables
- Roll meatballs
- Fill the pepper grinder with peppercorns as needed
- Pack and pound down kimchi and sauerkraut
- Make salsa
- Roll out crackers
- Cut apples for apple sauce
- Make chia jam
- Make gummies
- Watch younger siblings

Notes

-

Freezer & Batch Cooking Basics

Freezer cooking, is second only to planning ahead when it comes to successfully sticking with a dietary change, whether you're doing something strict like the Gut and Psychology Syndrome diet, or you're just eating grain-free when you're home, or you're trying to get more nutrient density in your meals by basing them on protein, fat and, vegetables rather than carbs.

Once it's a habit (it's a popular Sunday afternoon activity) it steamlines your life a bunch. It's also a great way to prepare for a new baby, a season of training for a sporting event, or for evenings when you work late.

Quality Over Quantity Kitchen Tools

One of the biggest time savers with freezer cooking is that you can use the same appliance the entire afternoon with only rinsing it between uses. One professional chef's knife, a high-quality food processor, nice large cutting board, excellent stock pots, and a durable cast iron skillet all get used nonstop all afternoon. Buying (or borrowing) equipment that isn't frustrating is efficient, and takes up much less counter space than a bunch of specialty gadgets.

Source Your Food Well

Since we're cooking so much at once, it's worth it to compare prices and quality of ingredients. If you can order your meat for pickup from a local farmer, they might put together a box that is exactly what you need. Some stores are going to have higher quality eggs or veggies at better prices, and others will be better for bulk spices and sea salt, and still others for canned goods and honey.

This is where I buy our groceries for freezer cooking here in Montana, it varies from location to location:

- Beef and Pork (local farm)
- Eggs, Greens, Squash, Onions, Cauliflower, Almond Flour, Chicken, Bacon, Butter, Fruit (Costco)
- Milk, Cream, Yogurt, Coconut Milk, Honey sometimes (Locally owned discount grocery store)
- Produce that Costco didn't have, misc meat that the local farm didn't have (Higher end locally owned grocery store in town)
- Spices, Herbs, and Salt (Mountain Rose Herbs)
- Coconut flakes, flour, and oil Tropical Traditions)

Streamline Your Kitchen

It may seem weird to scrub your kitchen just to go in and mess it up again, but starting with a sprakling clean work surface will make food prep easier and more enjoyable, and make cleanup at the end easier as well.

In addition to cleaning your kitchen, move any appliances (like the coffee maker) that you won't be using for bulk cooking, and keep the trash can out where it's near your work area, not in the cabinet.

Bring a gentle soap into the kitchen. Due to frequent hand washing between recipes, using dish soap will dry out your hands.

Finally, move any decorations that sit on the counter top – you'll want the largest work area available.

Enlist Help, If You Can

Even young children can help roll meatballs, scrub veggies, or unpack groceries. If you can get your kids to help, it not only helps you get things done quickly, but it also keeps them busy and from asking for your attention. When I have a job like this that is beyond normal chores, I do reward them with a prize for a job well done, this keeps them on task, and if they finish their task, it keeps them busy through the rest of my cooking time.

Popular in our home: Lego sets, a new app for the Kindle, Calvin and Hobbes books.

Use All Your Equipment At Once

When choosing what to cook next during your bulk cooking day, try to have all your appliances and pots in use at once, and try to order your cooking so that raw meat is done last because we have to wash everything it touches with hot water and soap, rather than just rinsing like we do with veggies.

Storing your Meals: Ditch the Plastic Guilt

Yes, I know that glass is the ideal thing to store food in. And for leftovers, or food that is going to be eaten within the next couple days I do use glass! But when it comes to freezing, I use plastic bags and containers due to their ability to lie flat or stack, and not shatter all over the kitchen if dropped. Frozen glass doesn't stack well, and is slippery and crazy brittle.

If you've been avoiding bulk cooking because you don't feel like you have the *best* containers to store your food in, consider getting rid of that guilt and giving yourself permission to make life a little easier.

When we bulk cook we are helping the environment even if we do use plastic bags by:

- Purchasing food in bulk, eliminating excess packaging
- Eliminating food waste due to veggies or meat going bad in the back of the fridge
- Using less water and electricity to wash dishes over and over again for each meal
- Reducing the amount of fuel needed to run to the grocery store for last minute food items during the dinner scramble.

And we're helping our health by having homemade well-sourced nutrient-dense meals easily, with much less stress.

Freeze flat

When possible, freeze your zip-top bags flat. If you live in a cool area and it's winter, you can even do this on the back porch (watch for animals – the neighborhood cats might take interest). Just lay the bags flat on the deck or on a table, and move to the freezer once frozen. Freezing flat helps keep the freezer organized.

Reheating Tips

Reheating the meals that we cook takes a little planning ahead, but it's easy to set aside 5 minutes in the morning to pull out a meal to thaw, or dump something in the crockpot.

I really like having a small crockpot so that I can have things like curry chicken once, without having to make enough for all week. Crockpots tend to burn things and cook unevenly unless they're 1/2 full, so a small crockpot can be a great investment. They don't cost that much either.

To thaw a meal when you forgot to pull something out in the morning, fill a large bowl or stock pot with barely warm water, and place the zip-top bag right in the water.

If you pull out a meal, and then don't end up using it, store it in the fridge in a bowl – that will contain any accidental leaks if the plastic bag was punctured a little bit sometime in the process. Then use within the next day or two.

American Favorites, Remade

Overview and Grocery List

We are making:

Dish	Meal	Quantity (serves 4)	Notes
Hamburgers	Main dish	4	Serve with squash fries
Jerky	Snack	6	Serve with fresh fruit
Sausage	Breakfast, main dish	6	Also used in pizza
Chicken Strips	Main dish	3	
Pizza	Main Dish	3	Allergen free option: Pizza Bake
Ketchup	Condiment	6	
Ranch	Condiment	6	Do not freeze- mayonnaise based
Pickles	Condiment	4 quarts	Lots of Probiotics!
Chicken Salad	Lunch, main dish	3	Do not freeze- mayonnaise based
Blueberry Jello	Treat	4	Healing benefits of gelatin!
Total:	16 main dishes	Plus treats, snacks, and condiments!	

Overview:

Spaghetti Squash & Chicken	Puncture Squash first	Bake Squash on oven rack, chicken in stock pot
Ground beef	Burgers	Mix and grill
	Jerky	Mix and dehydrate
	Breakfast Sausage	Mix and brown 1/3, shape the rest into patties and grill
Remove chicken	Add water	Simmer stock
Chicken strips	Toss with almond flour mixture	Bake in batches in oven. Remove spaghetti squash if soft.
Caulifower	Simmer 20 minutes	Cut squash fries while cooking
Squash fries	Peel, cut squash	Blanch after cauliflower (optional)
Chicken	Remove from stock	Cool chicken
Spaghetti Squash	Remove pulp	Put squash in bowls to cool
Condiments	Pickles, ketchup, ranch	Start condiments. Do between cauliflower mash and squash fries.
Spaghetti Squash	Make pizza (dairy and eggs) or Pizza Bake (Allergen Free)	
Chicken Salad	Mix chicken salad dressing	Chop and add chicken to mayo mixture once cool.
Blueberry Jello	Make	Make Jello while waiting for chicken to cool.

Equipment used:

Stock Pot Steam cauliflower for cauliflower mash.

Sauce Pan, medium. Ketchup and Blueberry Jello.

Dehydrator, Jerky. *Options: Can be done in oven after cooking day if you have oven jerky trays.*

Immersion Blender, Cauli Mash, Blueberry Jello. *Options: Can be done in batches in a regular blender.*

Blender, Mayonnaise. *Options: Can be done with an immersion blender or food processor.*

Mixing Bowls, 3, used throughout cooking day.

Baking Sheet, with shallow sides. Cook chicken nuggets and freeze pizza on to keep flat.

Colander, to rinse produce and drain squash.

Heavy Duty Vegetable Peeler, Peel butternut squash

Chef's Knife, used throughout cooking day

Cutting Board, large, used throughout.

Grocery List:

Meat

Ground beef, 9 lbs

[Burgers, 4 lbs]

[Jerky, 2 lbs]

[Breakfast Sausage, 3 lbs]

Chicken thighs, boneless skinless, 6 lbs

[Chicken Tenders]

Chicken, whole

[Stock, Ketchup, Chicken Salad]

Produce

Cauliflower, 6 lbs

Spaghetti Squash, 6 lbs (3 large)

Butternut Squash, 6-8 lbs (3-4 large)

Onions, white or yellow,

[Breakfast Sausage, 2-1/2]

Cucumbers, small pickling (sometimes called cocktail) 3-4 lbs

Blueberries, 3 cups

Garlic, 2 heads

Cauliflower, 4 lbs (or 2-3 heads)

[Garlic-Chive Cauliflower Mash]

Green onions, 1 bunch

[Chicken Salad]

Seasonings

Sea salt *(You will use more of this than you expect- buy at least 1/2 cup, if you find it in bulk bins there is usually substantial savigs by buying it there)*

Black pepper

Turmeric (optional)

Smoked Paprika

Basil

Parsley

Oregano

Dried Chives

Dill

Bay Leaf

Cinnamon

Pantry Items

Honey, 1 pint

Apple Cider Vinegar

Tomato sauce, or diced tomatoes, 24 ounces

[Pizza, or Pizza Bake]

Tomato Paste, 12 ounces

[Ketchup]

Avocado oil

Gelatin, 1 cup

[Broth Cubes]

[Blueberry Jello]

Almond Flour, 3 cups

[Chicken Tenders]

Other** Omit if you are dairy and/or egg free

Eggs, 2

[Pizza]

Cheese, gouda or mozzarella, 1 pound

[Pizza]

American Favorites, Remade - Recipes and Instructions

Spaghetti Squash Crust Pizza

Dairy Free: Use Spaghetti Pizza Bake Instructions

For the crust:

2-4 Spaghetti squash

--> Puncture squash and bake at 350* for 45 minutes, or until soft

---> Scoop out pulp

---> Use fork to separate strands, allow to cool until comfortable to touch so that it doesn't cook the eggs.

---> Add the following:

1 teaspoon sea salt

1/4 teaspoon freshly ground black pepper

1 pinch tumeric (optional)

2 eggs

1/4 cup shredded smoked gouda cheese

For the toppings:

Sugar free tomato sauce

2-3 cup shredded smoked gouda, or mozarella cheese

Any other pizza toppings of choice

Directions:

Use a fork to separate the spaghetti squash strands. Scoop the pulp into a very clean dish cloth or cheesecloth square and sprinkle with sea salt. Gather the cloth to make a ball of spaghetti squash, and then twist the top to squeeze out as much liquid as possible. This removes excess water and gives us a pizza crust that holds together.

After squeezing, turn the cloth inside out and dump the spaghetti squash into a bowl. Add pepper, tumeric, eggs, and 1/4 cup gouda cheese. Mix well with a fork.

Cover a baking sheet with parchment paper (don't skip this!) and press squash mixture into a crust shape.

Top with sauce, cheese, and toppings.

Freeze flat, on the parchment.

Spaghetti Squash Pizza Bake

Dairy and egg free

Tip: This is also a less time-consuming recipe than the pizza. It's delicious too!

2 large or 4 small spaghetti squash, cooked

4 cloves garlic, crushed

1 pound beef sausage, browned

2 cans diced tomatoes, drained, or 24 ounces tomato sauce

*Italian herbs of choice

Avocado oil to grease pans

Use 8x8 pans for 4-6 servings, loaf pans for 2-4 servings.

Mix spaghetti squash, garlic, sausage, tomatoes, and desired herbs. Grease pans with avocado oil. Place squash mixture into pans. Cover with foil, and freeze. For extra protection, slip into zip-top freezer bags.

To reheat: Thaw overnight or all day. Bake covered at 375* for 30 minutes, uncover and then bake another 15 minutes.

Tip: If you want to avoid the aluminum in these freezer pans while baking, simply pop the frozen casserole out like a big ice cube and place into a greased casserole dish and bake as indicated. This way you don't have to deal with bulky glass dishes in your freezer.

Chicken Stock & Cooked Chicken for Chicken Salad

We bake the chicken right in the stock pot. This gives more flavor and color to the chicken stock and the cooked chicken meat.

Ingredients:

1 Whole Chicken

--> Remove giblet package. Add chicken neck back in to pot.

--> Bake at 350* alongside the spaghetti squash for 30 minutes.

--> Add filtered water until covered by 1-2 inches

--> Simmer whole chicken for 45 minutes

--> Remove from heat, pour off chicken stock. Allow chicken to cool.

--> Using your fingers, remove all the meat from the chicken. Reserve cartridge, skin, and bones. Freeze for future broth.

Future broth directions: Using a large stock pot, place bones, drippings, and skin in. Break large bones to allow the nutritious marrow to get into the stock. Fill pot or slow cooker ¾ full with filtered water and add 1 teaspoon apple cider vinegar. Cook on medium-high until bubbling, then reduce heat to low and allow to simmer, covered, at least 8 hours. When done, allow to cool then pour stock through a strainer and transfer to mason jars to store in the fridge. Discard the remaining bones/skin in the pot.

To make easy broth cubes (homemade bouillon):

1. Start with your chicken stock – a gallon or more.

2. Reduce the gallon down to 2-3 cups by simmering with the lid off for 1-2 hours, or in a crock pot on high with the lid ajar to allow steam to escape for 5-6 hours.

3. Scoop out marrow from bones (break open chicken bones if using chicken) and add into reduced stock.

4. Add 1 tablespoon sea salt

5. Add 2/3 cup grassfed gelatin. This can be done when the stock is cool or warm.

6. Use an immersion blender to puree the marrow and thoroughly mix the gelatin.

7. Simmer again over medium-low heat until gelatin is melted in.

8. Remove from heat and chill 2+ hours. To save dishes, you can chill the mixture right in the stock pot.

9. Cut into 1″ cubes.

10. Transfer cubes to freezer bags, laying flat to freeze. They can be touching in places, but they're easier to get out individually if they are not completely touching. Once frozen, the bags can be stored upright or wherever they fit.

Hamburgers

--> Preheat griddle to medium heat

--> Mix:

4 lbs ground beef

2 teaspoons sea salt

3 cloves garlic, crushed

--> Form into patties

--> Grease griddle as needed with avocado oil

---> Cook patties for 5 minutes on each side- they will be browned, but not cooked through. This prevents them from becoming too dry when reheated.

Beef Breakfast Sausage

4 lbs of ground beef

2 teaspoons sea salt

1/2 teaspoon black pepper

2 onions, chopped finely

1/2 teaspoon of 3 different sweet spices (cinnamon, allspice, nutmeg, ginger etc)

1 teaspoon each of 3-4 savory spices (cumin, coriander, cayenne, sage, oregano, basil, paprika etc)

Tip: Like a little spice? Use 1 teaspoon of cayenne. Less spice? 1 teaspoon of paprika gives flavor and color without the heat

3 cloves garlic, crushed

[beef breakfast sausage cont]

--> Mix all ingredients together until spices are thoroughly mixed into the meat.

--> Shape 3/4 of the mixture into small patties and grill on griddle until undercooked (about 3 min on each side), so they can continue cooking when reheated.

--> Cook the remaining 1/4 of the mixture in a skillet, breaking up chunks, to add to **Spaghetti Squash Pizza** or (*dairy free*) **Spaghetti Squash Pizza Bake** for 10 minutes, or until browned through.

Ground Beef Jerky

3 pounds ground beef

2 tablespoons sea salt

1 teaspoon ground black pepper

1 teaspoon smoked paprika, or other spices as desired

--> In a bowl, mix seasonings into the beef until evenly distributed, with your hands. Divide beef mixture into 3 or 4 sections. Roll to the size of your dehydrator trays between either paraflex sheets or plastic wrap if you don't have paraflex sheets.

Remove plastic wrap, place on the dehydrator trays. Score into jerky-sized strips with a sharp knife, being careful not to cut the dehydrator tray, and dry on high overnight, or until thoroughly cooked. Break apart at the score lines.

Store in the fridge long term, though the salt and dehydrator preserve this well to last for a weekend camping trip or all day on a hike.

Baked Almond-Flour Crusted Chicken Tenders

6 pounds boneless chicken thighs

3 cup almond flour or almond meal

1 teaspoon salt

1/2 teaspoon black pepper

1 teaspoon Italian seasoning, or basil, parsley, or oregano

1 teaspoon paprika

Oil, tallow, or butter for greasing pan

Grease two 9x13-inch pans or a large cookie sheet with sides (to contain juices) with fat. Combine almond flour, salt, pepper and seasonings in a shallow bowl. Dip into almond flour mixture, pressing into the mixture on all sides so that it is covered. Lay chicken on cookie sheet.

Tip: If needed, you can do one batch, and then the next batch on the same cookie sheet after the first batch is done. Just coat the chicken with almond flour and leave it right in the almond flour bowl.

Repeat with remaining chicken pieces, placing them in a single layer. Touching is okay. Bake at 375 degrees Fahrenheit for 25 minutes or until chicken is slightly undercooked, but almond flour is golden. Chicken will continue cooking when re-heated.

---> Clean up now that we're moving onto veggies.

- Spray and wipe counters
- Load dishwasher and run the dishes used for meat

---> Take a 15-minute break if needed while the chicken strips cook.

---> Check spaghetti squash, is it soft? Is the skin starting to separate from the squash in places? Remove and allow to cool on the counter or on a platter.

---> Your chicken stock is still simmering on the stove top now.

---> Bring another stock pot filled 3/4 full with water to a boil over medium-high or high heat. This will cook your cauliflower for the cauli mash.

Squash Fries

Cut off the tops, and peel all butternut squash using a sturdy vegetable peeler. Cut into even fry-sized pieces.

Cut all the bulb ends last, scooping out pulp and cutting into wedges.

Garlic-Chive Cauliflower Mash

4 pounds cauliflower florets, or florets from 2 heads of cauliflower.

1/2 cup butter, coconut oil, or ghee

4 cloves garlic, crushed

1 tablespoon dried chives, or 1 bunch fresh, diced

1 tablespoon sea salt

Bring a large stock pot full of water to a boil. Add cauliflower and cook for 20 minutes. Once soft, drain and place in a large bowl while still hot. Add butter, garlic, chives, and sea salt. Puree with an immersion blender. Set aside to cool, and when comfortable to touch,

---> When pot of water comes to a boil, add cauliflower.

---> After cutting up the squash fries, the spaghetti squash should be cool enough to touch. Cut off ends, scoop out pulp, and use a fork to separate the spaghetti strands into a bowl. Continue to allow to cool.

Lacto-Fermented Dill Pickles

3-4 pounds small cucumbers

Or: 3-4 pounds large cucumbers cut into spears or rounds

4 teaspoons sea salt

1 bunch fresh dill or 1 tablespoon dried

2 tablespoons liquid from a previously successful ferment (optional)

Filtered water

[pickles, cont]

Rinse cucumbers. Evenly distribute between jars. If you have an extra jar, you will need more salt. Distribute dill between each jar, and add 1 teaspoon of sea salt per jar. Add 1 teaspoon (approx) pickle juice or other juice from previously successful ferment if using. Fill to within 1/2 inch of top of the jar with filtered water. Cover with air tight lid. Allow to culture on countertop in a cool-but-not-cold place for 5 days, transfer to fridge once pickles start to darken in color.

Easy Homemade Ketchup

12 ounces tomato paste

4 teaspoons apple cider vinegar

1-2 cups chicken stock as needed to thin

1/4 cup honey

½ teaspoon cinnamon

1/2 teaspoon sea salt (to taste)

1/2 teaspoon paprika

2 cloves garlic, crushed

1 bay leaf

Combine all ingredients except the bay leaf in a medium saucepan over medium high heat, bring to a boil, stirring often. Add in bay leaf , reduce heat to medium-low, and allow the ketchup to simmer for 20 minutes or until desired thickness. If it quickly gets too thick, add in more stock to thin. Remove bay leaf. Store in a quart jar, or freeze in half-cup containers if you don't use much ketchup.

---> As ketchup simmers, drain cauliflower.

---> After draining cauliflower, bring water in the same pot you boiled the cauliflower in to a boil to blanch squash fries. This step can be skipped if you plan on eating the squash fries within a month, but cooking time for the fries will be shortened and they will last longer in the freezer with the blanching step.

--> Turn heat off under chicken stock at this time too,

---> Make cauliflower mash.

---> Make spaghetti squash pizza crust OR spaghetti squash bake now that your spaghetti squash has cooled enough to handle.

---> Ketchup is done. Put in jar(s). Store in the fridge once cooled to room temperature.

---> Squash fries are blanching for 5-10 minutes, or until bright orange. This may need to be done in batches.

---> Remove chicken from chicken stock to cool. Continue with directions for broth cubes if desired, or place chicken stock in jars to store.

Blueberry Jello

3 cups fresh blueberries, rinsed (frozen, thawed can be used)

2 cups water

1/2 cup honey

1 lemon, juiced

1/4 cup gelatin

Directions: Combine all with an immersion blender in a medium sauce pan. Allow gelatin to absorb liquid for 5 minutes. Heat over medium heat for 5-10 minutes, or until all the gelatin is melted and mixture is hot but not boiling. Pour into a pie dish or similarly sized shallow container. Cool on the counter, and transfer to fridge to chill. Cut into squares once firm.

Make Mayonnaise:

2 eggs

2 cups avocado oil

1 teaspoon sea salt

Juice of 1 lemon, optional

Instructions: In a blender, or food processor whir the egg fors for 30 seconds to bring up to room temp. Add the oil slowly, taking a full 2 minutes to our it in. Add sea salt and lemon.

Ranch Dressing

1 cup homemade mayo

1 tablespoon dried chives

1 teaspoon dried parsley

2 cloves garlic, crushed

1/2 of a white onion, minced

Pinch of white pepper

1/2 teaspoon salt

Kefir or coconut milk as needed to thin

Directions:

Blend spices into 1 cup homemade mayonnaise. Add 1-4 tablespoons of kefir or coconut milk to reach desired consistency. Cover and refrigerate at least an hour, it's better if it sits overnight to meld the flavors.

Tip: Mayonnaise-based, so do not freeze

Chicken Salad

1 cup mayonnaise (the rest)

2 tablespoons mustard

1-2 cucumbers (the rest from the pickles)

2 cloves garlic

1/2 white oinion (left over from the ranch dressing)

1 bunch green onions, sliced into rounds, just the white and light green parts.

Salt and pepper to taste

1 whole chicken, cooked, chopped (from the chicken stock)

Mix all ingredients together. This does not freeze well, since it is mayonnaise based. Use for lunches this week.

--> Make chicken Salad. Store in fridge.

---> Chill Blueberry Jello and cut into squares once firm.

---> Dehydrate jerky for 4 hours. Once dry, break along scored lines and store in a zip-top bag in the fridge or freezer.

Storage and Reheating Instructions

Spaghetti Squash Pizza

To store: Freeze flat on parchment paper. Keep pizza on cardboard or a baking sheet (under the parchment) while freezing so that it stays flat. Once frozen solid, place in a gallon zip-top bag, press out air, and the pizza can be stacked.

Use within:6 months.

Reheat: Keep on parchment paper to bake. Can be baked from frozen, or thawed on a cookie sheet prior to baking. Bake at 425* for 35 minutes from frozen, 25 if thawed, or until cheese is bubbly and crust is turning golden brown around the edges.

Serving suggestions: Serve with carrot sticks and ranch dressing to dip.

Chicken Stock

To Store: If made into broth cubes, transfer broth cubes into zip-top bag once firm and freeze. If not made into broth, keep in a jar with a lid in the fridge.

Use within: 6 months if frozen, 3 weeks if liquid.

Reheat: Use as chicken broth in recipes.

Serving Suggestions:Quick soup: Fill a saucepan with frozen veggies. Add chicken stock to cover and 1 teaspoon sea salt. Simmer until veggies are starting to soften. Add in 1 cup cooked meat, cut into small cubes. Enjoy!

Ranch Dressing

To Store: Store in the fridge in a covered container. Do not freeze.

Use within:3 weeks.

Serving Suggestions: Put in a small squeeze container for children's lunches!

Blueberry Jello

To Store: Freeze flat in zip-top bags or keep covered in the fridge.

Use within:6 Months frozen, 1 week in the refrigerator.

Reheat: Thaw if needed, overnight, keep in the fridge.

Serving Suggestions: Use as a treat or a snack.

Spaghetti Squash Pizza Bake

To Store: Freeze in baking pans, slip baking pans into a zip-top bag for storage longer than one week.

Use within: 6 months.

Reheat: Thaw overnight in the fridge. Transfer to the oven (will still be partially frozen) and bake at 350* covered, until cooked through- about 45 minutes. Remove cover and bake an additional 15 minutes.

Serving Suggestions: Leftovers make a great lunch the next day!

Chicken Salad

To Store: Keep covered in the refrigerator.

Use within: 1 week.

Reheat: Not needed, though you can use it for patty melts over mushrooms, tomatoes, or other sliced, flat veggies. Just pile it on top of the veggie, put on a metal baking dish, and heat under the broiler!

Notes: This is a great lunch!

Hamburgers

To Store: Freeze flat in zip-top bags or keep covered in the fridge.

Use within:6 Months frozen, 1 week in the refrigerator.

Reheat: Thaw overnight in the fridge or a couple hours on the counter. Grill on a dry grill or with a little fat over medium heat until cooked through, about 5-7 minutes on each side.

Serving Suggestions: Top with guacamole, ketchup, ranch dressing, and bacon for a special treat.

Breakfast Sausage

To Store: Keep covered in the fridge. Or lay flat to freeze in a zip-top bag.

Use within: 1 week in the fridge, 6 months frozen.

Reheat: Microwave if desired, or heat in skillet over medium heat until heated through, about 5 minutes on each side.

Serving Suggestions: Perfect with eggs, sliced fruit, or on it's own!

Chicken Tenders

To Store: Freeze flat in zip-top bags.

Use within:6 Months frozen.

Reheat: Heat in the toaster oven or regular oven on a baking sheet at 375* for 10-15 minutes, or until hot all the way through.

Serving Suggestions: Served with ketchup and pickles and fruit for dessert. These go well in lunches too, just make sure they are all the way cooked before putting into lunches.

Beef Jerky

To Store: Keep in a lidded container in the fridge.

Use within: 6 Months when kept in the fridge or freezer. Can stay out for a couple days (ie camping or backpacking) and it will be fine.

Reheat: Not needed. Will thaw quickly from the freezer.

Serving Suggestions: Beef jerky is great road trip food, and also great when you need quick protein in the morning before a workout. It's also great to dip! Dip in ranch dressing, guacamole, or your favorite dip.

Squash Fries

To Store: Freeze flat in zip-top bags. If you remember, once they have started to freeze (after about 2-3 hours) gently flip the bag a few times to help separate the fries.

Use within: 6 months.

Reheat: Pull out desired amount. Place in shallow baking dish (8x8 pan or pie plate works well). Bake at 375* for 20-30 minutes or until hot and the edges are starting to crisp.

Serving Suggestions: Goes great with burgers!

Cauliflower Mash

To Store: Place desired amount in zip-top bags (I like the quart size).

Use within: 6 Months.

Reheat: Thaw in the fridge or counter on a pie plate or similar dish to catch any drips. Bake in a shallow casserole dish, uncovered, alongside dinner. From thawed, this will take about 30 minutes. Temp is flexible (from 350*-425* is fine)

Serving Suggestions: This 'mashed potato' remake is delicious on its own. For a different take, add 2 cups of chicken stock and 1/2 teaspoon sea salt to about 1 quart of cauliflower mash for a quick soup. Can be cooked low all day in the slow cooker. Top with bacon bits or crumbled sausage.

Pickles

To Store: After initial fermentation, 'burp' your ferment (unscrew lid, and allow excess air to escape- do this over the sink) and then store in the fridge.

Use within: Once you start using a ferment, you introduce bacteria every time you open the jar, so try to use the jar within 10 days of first use. Otherwise, unopened (after the initial 'burping') ferments will stay in the fridge for 6 months or longer.

Reheat: Keep raw to keep enzymes and probiotics intact.

Serving Suggestions: Serve alongside all meals as a condiment to provide needed probiotics. You may be surprised- children often LOVE ferments!

Ketchup

To Store: Cover and keep in the fridge. You can rinse out an old ketchup container and use that, just be sure to keep it in the refrigerator rather than the cupboard. Can be frozen in zip-top bags or small plastic containers, just allow for a little expansion when freezing (leave 1 inch of room at the top of the container).

Use within:1 week. Can be frozen for 6 months.

Serving Suggestions: This can be put in small containers and added to packed lunches- kids love it!

Freezer to Slow Cooker

Overview and Grocery List

Start Chicken Stock	Oven Proof Stock Pot	Rinse apples and pears
Apple Chutney	Cutting Board, Quart Jars	
Apple-Pear Sauce		Preheat griddle for Beef and Pork
Brown Beef Ribs	Griddle	
Brown Pork Chops	Griddle	Remove Chicken Stock from Oven if browned
Bake Bacon	Baking Sheet	Continue browning beef and pork
Homemade Ketchup	Sauce Pan	Will be used with beef ribs
Salsa	Quart jars	Will be used for Moroccan chicken and to ferment
Stir Ketchup, thin as needed	Add water to chicken and simmer for stock	Continue browning pork and beef, set aside as browned on each side, Bacon may be done
Roasted Brussels	Use same baking sheet as the bacon	Pork and beef will be done soon. Leave griddle out.
Moroccan Chicken	Saucepan	Grill onions and mushrooms for Pork and Beef dishes
Cauliflower rice	Food processor- grating attachment	Also used for stuffed peppers
Stuffed Peppers	Disposible 8x8 containers	Roasted brussels will be ready while you're doing this, set aside to cool
Assemble Pork Chops	Assemble Beef Ribs	Assemble Moroccan Chicken
Stuffed Apples		Start Elderberry Gummies now too
Elderberry Gummies	Saucepan	
You're done!		Lay flat to freeze- this will keep your freezer so much more organized

Grocery List

Meat

2 pounds bone-in Chicken (thighs, wings, backs)

   [Chicken stock and broth cubes]

Bacon, 2 lbs

   [Baked Bacon, grease used in Brussels]

Beef Short ribs, 12-16

[Melt-in-Mouth Beef Short Ribs]

Beef or pork, ground, 4 lbs

[Stuffed Peppers]

Pork Loin Chops, Bone in, 12 (1 inch thick+)

[Pork Chops with Tomatoes and Mushrooms]

Chicken Thighs, Boneless/Skinless, 4 lbs

[Moroccan Chicken]

Produce

Apples, 10 lbs Red Delicious {any kind is fine}

[Apple chutney, 6 ea]

[Apple-Pear Sauce, the rest]

Apples, 5 lbs Granny Smith {Needs to be tart and firm}

[Stuffed Apples]

Pears, 5 lbs {Can use peaches, plums, or more apples, or omit}

[Apple-Pear Sauce]

Lemons, 2

[Apple Chutney, 2]

Jalapeno, 1

[Salsa, Moroccan Chicken, 1]

Chilies, Anaheim, 4 (also called California chilies)

[Salsa, Moroccan Chicken, 2]

[Stiffed bell peppers, 2]

Garlic, 3 heads

Onions, yellow, 6

[Beef Ribs, 4 med]

[Salsa/Moroccan Chicken, 2]

Tomatoes, Roma, 8

[Salsa, Moroccan Chicken]

Mushrooms, 1 pound (any kind)

[Pork Chops]

Bell Peppers, any color, 15

[Pork Chops, 3]

[Stuffed Peppers, 12]

Brussels Sprouts, 2 lbs

[Roasted Brussels Sprouts]

Cauliflower, 4 Lbs

[Stuffed peppers, 1 lb]

[Cauliflower Rice, 3 lbs]

Fresh Herbs

(*Dried can be substituted for all- use 1/4 the amount of dried*)

Cilantro, 1 bunch

Parsley, 1/4 cup flat leaf

Oregano, 1 small bunch

Seasonings

Sea salt (*You will use more of this than you expect- buy at least 1/2 cup, if you find it in bulk bins there is usually substantial savings by buying it there*)

Black pepper

Bay Leaf

Fennel seeds

Cinnamon

Cloves, ground

Paprika

Oregano

Basil

Pantry Items

Honey, 1 pint

[Apple chutney, Beef Ribs, Superhero Gummies]

Raisins, 3 cups

[Apple Chutney, 1/2 cup]

[Moroccan Chicken, 1/4 cup]

[Stuffed apples, ~ 2 cups]

Coconut Oil, 1 pint

Apple Cider Vinegar

Tomato paste, 24 ounces

[Beef Short Ribs, 12 oz]

[Stuffed Peppers, 12 oz]

Tomato Sauce, 32 ounces

[Pork Chops]

Watch for added sugar and soy

Yellow Mustard

Tart Cherry Juice, 3 cups

[Superhero Gummies]

Gelatin, 1/2 cup

[Gummies] * The orange/red can of Great Lakes brand, NOT the green can

Other

Kombucha, 2 tablespoons (store bought or homemade)

[Apple Chutney]

Elderberry capsules, berries and flowers, 10 capsules

[Gummies]

Freezer-to-Slow Cooker Instructions and Recipes

Chicken Stock & Broth Cubes

2 lbs Drumsticks, Bone-in Thighs, or Wings

--> Bake chicken in stock pot at 400*

--> Rinse all apples/pears with a water and a few tablepoons apple cider vinegar

Apple Chutney

Approx 6 Apples

--> Chop apples (skin on) to fill 3 quart jars

Add to each jar:

Juice of 2 lemons

2 tablespoons honey

2 tablespoons kombucha to start culture

1/2 cup raisins

2 inches of hot chili pepper, fresh and de-seeded

1 teaspoon fennel seeds

1 teaspoon cinnamon

1 teaspoon cloves, ground

--> Pack gently to start to release the juices. If needed, add filtered water to cover the fruit.

---> Cover and leave at room temperature for 2 days, transferring to the refrigerator for up to 2 months.

--> Discard the chili pepper before consuming.

Apple-Pear Sauce

Core and chop, but do not peel the rest of the apples and pears.

Place into zip-top bags. If being used within 2 months, these bags of apples will hold up just fine in the freezer (usually you need to blanch produce before it goes in the freezer to maintain texture and flavor).

To cook: Gently drop bag on counter to break up apple/pear chunks. Pour into slow cooker until cooker is 75% to 100% full. Add 1 cup filtered water and a sprinkle of cinnamon if desired. Cook on low for 6-10 hours, high for 4-6 hours, and then puree with an immersion blender. Delicious, easy, and healthy whole-fruit apple-pear sauce!

--> Heat griddle to medium-high heat to sear pork chops and beef ribs

Baked Bacon

--> Bake alongside chicken baking for stock

2 lbs bacon

---> Lay bacon flat, touching but not overlapping, on a cookie sheet with sides to contain juices.

---> Bake at 400* for 25 minutes, or until cooked through.

--> To store, keep covered or in a zip-top bag in the fridge or freezer.

--> To reheat, heat in a pan for 3 minutes over medium heat, or in the toaster oven for 10 minutes. Microwave for 30 seconds on high.

Melt-in-Your-Mouth Beef Short Ribs

(makes 3-4 dinners)

12-16 pounds beef short ribs

4 tablespoons butter, olive oil, avocado oil, or coconut oil

4 medium yellow onions

1 recipe homemade ketchup (recipe to follow)

1/2 cup apple cider vinegar

1/2 cup honey

--> Sear short ribs on the griddle for 5 minutes on each side over medium-high heat, or until starting to brown.

--> Set ribs aside to cool.

Homemade ketchup

(used in the short ribs)

12 ounces tomato paste

4 teaspoons apple cider vinegar

1 teaspoon yellow mustard

1 cup stock

1/4 cup honey

½ teaspoon cinnamon

½ teaspoon sea salt (to taste)

¼ teaspoon paprika

2 cloves garlic, crushed

1 bay leaf

Combine all ingredients except the bay leaf in a medium saucepan over medium high heat, bring to a boil, stirring often. Add in bay leaf , reduce heat to medium-low, and allow the ketchup to simmer for 20 minutes or until desired thickness. If it quickly gets too thick, add in more stock to thin. Remove bay leaf.

---> Turn Beef Ribs

---> Check bacon, remove from oven and put in another layer to bake if first batch is done.

Homemade Salsa

This is made to ferment, and for the Moroccan Chicken

1 Jalapeno

2 Anaheim chilies

1 bunch cilantro

8 Roma tomatoes

2 white or yellow onions

2 tablespoons sea salt.

--> Rinse jalapeno, chilies, cilantro, and tomatoes.

--> Peel onions, dice.

---> Remove stems and rinse out seeds from peppers, dice.

--> Chop Cilantro leaves, discard stems.

---> Chop tomatoes

Pork Chops with Tomatoes and Mushrooms

12 Thick Bone-in Pork Loin Chops (1 inch +)

1 pound mushrooms, sliced

3Bell peppers, cut into rounds

3 cloves garlic

32 ounces tomato sauce

1/4 cup minced flat-leaf parsley

1 teaspoon dried oregano

1 teaspoon dried basil

1/2 teaspoon sea salt

---> Continue flipping the pork chops when done

--> Continue stirring ketchup

---> Remove the chicken once browned in the oven, add water until pot is 3/4 full, and then simmer on stovetop over medium-low heat.

---> Back to the salsa, layer chopped tomatoes, onions, peppers and cilantro, onions, and tomatoes again into 2 quart jars.

---> Pound down with a smaller mason jar, or the handle of a wooden spoon, and add more tomatoes until full, continuing to pound down.

--> Add 1 tablespoon sea salt per quart jar to salsa. Screw lid on tight. One quart will be used for the Moroccan Chicken, the other will be fermented salsa.

--> Remove baked bacon from oven. Allow to cool for a few minutes.

--> Turn off heat under ketchup.

Roasted Brussels Sprouts

We use the bacon grease to roast the brussels in, it's the most delicious way to eat these nutrient-rich green veggies.

2 pounds Brussels sprouts

--> Rinse brussels sprouts. Trim stem ends if needed.

--> Remove bacon to cool further.

--> Pour off most of the bacon grease (save to cook with), but leave a couple tablespoons on the baking sheet.

--> Place brussels on baking sheet, and give a shake to coat more evenly. Sprinkle with 1 teaspoon sea salt (or to taste) and place in the oven that is at 400* still from the bacon. Roast for 25 minutes.

Cauliflower Rice

(*at this time we will rice cauliflower for the stuffed peppers as well*)

4 lbs cauliflower florets

--> In a food processor with a grating attachment, grate (rice) cauliflower, emptying the bowl of the food processor as needed.

Stuffed Bell Peppers

2 Anaheim Chilies

--> Rinse out seeds

1 small bunch fresh oregano, leaves only (or 1 teaspoon dried)

12 Bell Peppers, any color

---> Fit food processor with chopping blade.

---> Remove tops from peppers, rinse out seeds and use fingers to remove membranes.

---> Pulse: Tops of the peppers, chilies, and oregano until finely chopped. Add to the reserved cauliflower.

6 cloves garlic

---> Crush, add to cauliflower mixture

12 Ounces tomato paste

--> Add to cauliflower mixture

*--> Check brussels, remove from oven, and allow to cool.

4 Lbs Ground beef, pork, or a combination of the two

3 teaspoons sea salt

---> Mix all together with your hands in the bowl you put the cauliflower mixture into.

--> Set 4 bell pepper 'bowls' into each 8x8 or similarly sized oven-proof containers (makes 3 pans with 4 peppers each)

---> Pack peppers full of meat mixture.

---> Bake peppers in the oven at 350* for 25 minutes to start to cook. They will continue cooking when reheated. Cooking keeps the peppers from breaking down in the freezer. You can skip this if you plan to use these this week.

Continue with...

--> Package roasted brussels sprouts in zip-top bag. Freeze flat.

---> Label freezer bags: 3 Moroccan Chicken, 3 Stuffed Peppers, 3 Short ribs, 3 Pork Chops

Moroccan Chicken

6 cloves garlic, crushed

1 quart salsa

1/4 cup raisins

1/4 cup honey (optional)

--> Heat in saucepan over medium heat until cooked down

4 lbs Boneless/Skinless Chicken Thighs

Continue with...

---> Onions and mushrooms for pork chops and beef ribs, chop, grill

---> Assemble rib and pork chop packs in zip-top bags: Divide ingredients evenly across the bags.

--> Assemble Moroccan chicken in zip-top bags: Evenly distribute chicken across 3 bags, evenly distribute salsa mixture over the top after allowing it to cool.

You can be done now if needed

Running out of steam? Call it a great day! Your main dishes and veggie sides are complete! The last two sweet recipes take about half an hour longer to complete, if you can they're delicious too :)

Stuffed Apples

5 lbs granny smith apples

2 cups raisins

1/4 cup butter or coconut oil

--> Use the circular part of a vegetable peeler to core the center of the apples, leaving a small piece in the bottom (don't push it all the way through). A butter knife can be used to 'drill' out the center once it's started with the peeler.

--> Cut butter into 1/2 teaspoon pieces, and stuff one piece of butter into the apple, then stuff the rest of the way with raisins. Sprinkle with cinnamon if desired.

--> Place in freezer bag and freeze in a single layer. They keep for about one month in the freezer, since they are not pre-baked and the enzymes are still active. To keep longer, pre-bake for 20 minutes at 350*, allow to cool, then place in your freezer bag. These can be baked, covered, for an hour alongside dinner (350-425) or stacked in the slow cooker and cooked on low for 6 hours, high for 3. They can be placed in the slow cooker still frozen.

Superhero Gummies

3 cups tart cherry juice

1/2 cup gelatin

1/4 cup honey (to taste)

10 capsules elderberry

Open the capsules, and put the contents of the capsules in a sauce pan, discard the actual capsule.

Combine all ingredients in a small sauce pan, mix well with a fork. Heat over medium heat until gelatin turns clear, stirring every few minutes, about 5-10 minutes. Grease a glass or other smooth-sided loaf pan or small dish lightly with coconut oil. Pour clear mixture into loaf pan, allow to cool down to room temp on the counter so you don't warm up your fridge too much, then cover with plastic wrap and allow to chill in the fridge.

To cut into gummies, use a butter knife to loosen the large gummie block from the container onto a cutting board, and cut into cubes with a butcher knife. These last for about 10 days in the fridge, covered, or 6 months in the freezer.

Notes:

Freezer-to-Slow Cooker Storage and Reheating Instructions

Chicken Stock

To store: Store broth cubes (if made) in a zip-top bag in the freezer. Store liquid broth in quart mason jars in the fridge.

Use within: 6 months for the broth cubes, 3 weeks for the broth in the fridge.

Tips: Add 1 quart broth or 4 broth cubes + 3/1/2 cups filtered water to one medium saucepan filled with vegetables. Simmer for 30 minute, add 1 teaspoon sea salt, and there is a delicious fast soup!

Reheat: Heat on stove. Can be microwaved if you wish.

Serving suggestions: In addition to soups, broth is a delicious hot drink, just add a pinch of sea salt. Use as the liquid in any savory dishes (can replace water).

Apple Chutney

To Store: After initial fermentation, 'burp' your ferment (unscrew lid, and allow excess air to escape- do this over the sink) and then store in the fridge.

Use within: Once you start using a ferment, you introduce bacteria every time you open the jar, so try to use the jar within 10 days of first use. Otherwise, unopened (after the initial 'burping') ferments will stay in the fridge for 6 months or longer.

Reheat: Keep raw to keep enzymes and probiotics in tact.

Serving Suggestions: Serve alongside all meals as a condiment to provide needed probiotics. You may be surprised- children often LOVE ferments!

Apple-Pear Sauce

To Store: Freeze in zip-top bags, laying flat to freeze and being careful not to crush. You want to be able to pour out your desired amount of apple/pear pieces to make fast delicious apple-pear sauce.

Use within: 2 months.

Reheat: Pour desired amount of frozen fruit pieces into a slow cooker or sauce pan that has a lid. If using a slow cooker, make sure it is at least 2/3 full. Sauce will reduce by about half as it cooks.

Add 1/2 cup of water, and cook in the slow cooker on low for 8 hours or place the lid on the saucepan and cook on medium, reducing the heat to med-low for an additional 45 minutes.

Puree with an immersion blender before serving.

Serving Suggestions: Melt a few tablespoons of butter into your sauce to help balance all the sugar in the fruit. Serve alongside meat, roast, or really any meal!

Fermented Salsa

To Store: After initial fermentation, 'burp' your ferment (unscrew lid, and allow excess air to escape- do this over the sink) and then store in the fridge.

Use within: Once you start using a ferment, you introduce bacteria every time you open the jar, so try to use the jar within 10 days of first use. Otherwise, unopened (after the initial 'burping') ferments will stay in the fridge for 6 months or longer.

Reheat: Keep raw to keep enzymes and probiotics in tact.

Serving Suggestions: Serve alongside Mexican dishes, over eggs, with beans, or over any plain meat.

Melt-In-Your-Mouth Beef Ribs

To Store: Freeze flat in zip-top bags.

Use within:6 Months.

Reheat: Thaw overnight in the fridge. Dish will still be partially frozen in the morning. Place in medium slow cooker and cook on low 8-10 hours, or high for 4-5 hours.

Serving Suggestions: Spoon liquid and vegetables from the slow cooker over the ribs. Serve with cauliflower rice and apple chutney.

Cauliflower Rice

To Store: Freeze in zip-top bags. Do not crush. Freeze flat, and flip and gently break up clumps after being in the freezer about 3 hours. This will keep it 'pourable'.

Use within: 6 weeks.

Reheat: Sautee in a fat (butter, tallow, lard) over medium-high heat. From frozen this takes about 15 minutes. Add salt to taste.

Serving Suggestions: Use alongside meat dishes in place of traditional rice.

Pork Chops with Tomato and Mushrooms

To Store: Freeze flat in zip-top bags.

Use within:6 Months.

Reheat: Thaw overnight in the fridge. Dish will still be partially frozen in the morning. Place in medium slow cooker and cook on low 8-10 hours, or high for 4-5 hours.

Serving Suggestions: Spoon liquid and vegetables from the slow cooker over the pork chops. Serve with cauliflower rice and a fresh green salad.

Roasted Brussels Sprouts

To Store: Freeze in a zip-top bag.

Use within: 6 months.

Reheat: Thaw. Sautee in a little fat over medium heat or microwave.

Serving Suggestions: These roasted Brussels are a great side dish for a meat dish. They also can be added to simmering soup.

Moroccan Chicken

To Store: Freeze flat in zip-top bags.

Use within:6 Months.

Reheat: Thaw overnight in the fridge. Dish will still be partially frozen in the morning. Place in small or medium slow cooker and cook on low 8-10 hours, or high for 4-5 hours.

Serving Suggestions: Spoon liquid and vegetables from the slow cooker over the ribs. Serve with cauliflower rice and fermented salsa.

Stuffed Peppers

To Store: Freeze in zip-top bags.

Use within:6 Months.

Reheat: Remove desired peppers, and place in a slow cooker, they can be stacked if needed. They can be cooked directly from frozen, it will take the higher end of the cooking time, or place in the slow cooker to thaw the night before, and shorten the cooking time. Cook on low 8-10 hours, or high for 4-5 hours.

Can also be baked. Thaw in a baking dish upright (a casserole dish with a lid works well) and bake covered at 350* until heated through, about 45 minutes.

Serving Suggestions: Top with sour cream, shredded cheese, and fresh herbs or fermented salsa.

Elderberry Gummies

To Store: Keep covered with plastic wrap in the fridge.

Use within: 10 days.

Reheat: Not needed.

Serving Suggestions: Serve as dessert or a treat.

Stuffed Apples

To Store: Store in 2-3 gallon zip-top bags. Do not pack the bags too full, and do not squash in the freezer.

Use within:3 months.

Reheat: Bake in a covered casserole from frozen 90 minutes, or thawed 45-60 minutes, until soft. In the slow cooker, stack frozen apples and cook on low for 6-8 hours or high for 3 hours.

Serving Suggestions: Top with yogurt, coconut milk, and a sprinkle of cinnamon. Delicious for dessert or a warm breakfast or snack.

Bonus: Soup Packs

These soup packs make it a snap to make soup for either main dishes, or a side dish or starter. This is a fantastic way to get broth in your diet for easy-to-absorb amino acids, and tons of vegetables for vitamins, minerals, and fiber. Plus they are gorgeous.

Follow these directions to make 6 different soups that would feed a family of 4. If you want to cook less at a time, simply make the same amount, but use quart zip-top bags rather than gallon bags.

Ingredients/Grocery List

1 pot chicken or beef stock (you made a pot of stock in the Freezer-to-Slow Cooker Class, which is perfect for this. If you don't have that any more, you will need to make more prior to starting. See instructions in the Freezer-to-Slow Cooker class)

1 cup Grassfed Beef Gelatin

A combination of vegetables that are in season, inexpensive, and your family's preference.

Used in this example:

4 butternut squash

6-10 onions

1 bunch celery

6 Anaheim chilies

5-10 lbs carrots

Also good (5 lbs is a good amount): Broccoli, cauliflower, summer squash, green beans, celery root, beets.

Seasonings:

1/4 cup sea salt

Smoked Paprika

Cayenne Pepper

Basil

Oregano

Granulated Garlic

Ginger

Directions

- Reduce stock to 2-3 quarts.
- Allow stock to cool.
- Once cooled to room temp, add gelatin and mix in with a whisk or fork. Allow gelatin to absorb liquid.
- Preheat oven to 425* If you have a convection oven, use the convection setting.
- Peel and chop onions.
- Rinse, deseed, and chop peppers.
- Place chopped onions and peppers on a baking sheet, sprinkle with about 1 tablespoon sea salt.
- Roast onions and peppers in the oven.
- Once gelatin has absorbed the stock and is thick, heat over medium-low heat for 15 minutes, or until melted.
- Continue rinsing, peeling, and chopping other vegetables.
- Once gelatin is melted, remove from heat and allow to cool. Transfer to fridge once close to room temperature (or cover and place outside where the cold winter air can cool it for free!)
- Roast the rest of the vegetables in shallow pans or dishes in the same manner as the onions and peppers. Roast with similar colors together.
- Once vegetables are starting to brown at the edges (about 20 minutes of roasting),

remove from oven and put new vegetables in until all vegetables have been roasted.

- Allow vegetables to cool.
- Once gelatin/broth mixture is solidified, cut into 2"x2" squares.
- Transfer vegetables to bags in desired amounts and combinations and add 1 tablespoon of salt and ½-1 teaspoon of 2-3 of the seasonings, in different combinations.
- Add one-two broth cubes to each bag.
- Add 1 teaspoon fine sea salt or 2 teaspoons coarse sea salt to each gallon bag as you add the broth cube.

Reheating instructions (all soups):

- Fill a saucepan, stock pot, or crock pot ½ to ¾ full with vegetables and broth cube from the soup pack.
- Cover frozen vegetables with filtered water.
- **Slow cooker:** Cook on low for 8-10 hours, high for 4-6.
- **Stove top:** Cook over medium heat, covered, until brought to a simmer. Reduce heat to low and cook an additional 30 minutes, until heated through.

Flavor combinations and serving instructions:

*** Add 1 teaspoon fine sea salt or 2 teaspoons coarse sea salt to each gallon bag as you add the broth cube. Add more salt after cooking, to taste.

Curried Butternut Squash:

1 part onion
4 parts butternut squash
1 teaspoon ginger
1 tablespoon granulated garlic
Top with coconut milk after pureeing.

Classic Chicken Soup:
1 part each of the vegetables
1 tablespoon dried basil
1 teaspoon dried oregano

1 pound boneless/skinless chicken, or 2 cups leftover cooked chicken.

After cooking, do not puree.

Add 2 cups cooked, diced chicken during the last 20 minutes of cooking. Squeeze the juice of 1/2 fresh lemon over each bowl.

French Onion Soup

3 parts onions

Optional: 1 part green beans

Garnish with shredded parmesan, if you eat dairy, to serve.

Carrot-Butternut Soup

2 parts roasted carrots
2 parts roasted butternut squash
1 part onions
1 teaspoon smoked paprika

Cook, then puree with an immersion blender.

Top with a sprinkle of paprika and dollop of yogurt before serving.

Cream of Celery

2 parts celery

1 part onions

1/2 teaspoon dried coriander OR thyme

Puree this soup after cooking. Garnish with sour cream or coconut milk.

Ginger Beef

1 part onions

2 parts carrots (if you did broccoli and/or cauliflower, use in place of the carrots)

1 inch fresh ginger, grated, or 1/2 teaspoon powdered ginger

To serve:

1/2 teaspoon freshly ground black pepper

Pinch sea salt

1 pound grassfed beef steak

1 tablespoon tallow, butter, ghee, or coconut oil

Half an hour before dinner, season the beef with salt and pepper and cook over medium-high heat for 5 minutes in a skillet in melted fat. Flip over once browned, reduce heat to medium-low, and then continue cooking until cooked through (10-15 minutes- it will depend on the thickness of your steak)

Allow to rest for 10 minutes, then dice. Puree soup with an immersion blender, and then add beef and serve.

Cozy Winter Suppers

Overview and Grocery List

We are making

Vegetable/side	Protein/Main	Treat	Sauce
Roasted Root Veg (4)	Meatloaf (4)		
Mashed Squash (4)	Brazilian Chicken (4)	OJ Gummies	Spinach Artichoke
Cauli rice or mashed cauli (3)	Meatballs (4)	Crackers	Beet Kvass, 1 quart
Sauerkraut (2 quarts)			

Overview

Make broth	Stovetop	
Puncture squash	Bake	
Orange Juice Gummies	Juice oranges, mix ingredients	Saucepan
Sunflower seed crackers	Food processor	Wash food processor
Shred mushrooms for meatloaf	Shred veg for meatballs	Rinse food processor
Make meatballs	Shallow pan	Cook mushrooms and onions
Roasted Root Vegetables	Shallow dish(s)	Make Beet Kvass as you cut up root veg.
Brazilian Chicken	Can be pre-baked or frozen seasoned	
Bacon-wrapped meatloaf		
Sauerkraut	Food processor	Rinse food processor for spinach dip
Boil/steam cauliflower for mashed cauliflower		Stock pot, immersion blender
Spinach artichoke dip	Food processor	First make mayo, then add spinach ingredients
Cut up OJ Gummies that have chilled now	Culture sauerkraut for 5+ days	Freeze/Store
Done!		

Grocery List

Meat

Beef, ground, 4 lbs

[Bacon-Wrapped Meatloaf]

Pork, ground, 2-3 lbs (can sub any ground meat)

[Bacon Wrapped Meatloaf]

[Asian-Style Meatballs]

Bacon, 2 lbs (can use beef bacon)

[Bacon-Wrapped Meatloaf]

Chicken, bone-in, skin on, 1 lb

[Stock]

Chicken, boneless, skinless thighs, 5 lbs

[Brazilian Chicken Bites]

Turkey, ground, 3 lbs

[Asian-Style Meatballs]

Produce

Onions, large yellow or white, 5

[Bacon-Wrapped Meatloaf]

[Sautéed Mushrooms and Onions]

Onions, green, 1 bunch

[Asian-Style Meatballs]

Mushrooms, white button (or any kind), 16 oz

[Bacon-Wrapped Meatloaf]

[Sautéed Mushrooms and Onions]

Hard Winter Squash (recommend butternut), 6-12

[Mashed Salt and Pepper Squash]

Cauliflower Florets (2-3 heads), 4-6 lbs

[Cauli Chive Mash]

Cabbage, 1 head, red or purple

[Sauerkraut]

Beets, 1 bunch

[Roasted Vegetables]

Carrots, 5 lbs

[Roasted Vegetables]

Radishes, 8 oz

[Roasted Vegetables]

Garlic, 2 heads

[Multiple recipes]

Ginger, 1/2 inch fresh

[Asian-Style Meatballs]

Oranges, 6-10 (to make 3 C juice)

[OJ Gummies]

Spinach, 6 cups

[Spinach Artichoke Dip]

Seasonings

Sea salt *(You will use more of this than you expect- buy at least 1/2 cup, if you find it in bulk bins there is usually substantial savings by buying it there)*

Cumin

Coriander

Turmeric

Paprika

Cayenne

Black or White Pepper

Chives, dried, 1 tablespoon

Sage

Pantry Items

Gelatin, 1 cup (Great Lakes or Perfect Supplements Brand, NOT collagen)

[OJ Gummies]

Honey, 1/2 cup

[OJ Gummies]

Fish Sauce

[Asian-Style Meatballs]

Coconut Aminos, 1/4 cup

[Asian-Style Meatballs]

Sunflower Seeds, 1 cup

Sesame Seeds, 1 cup

[Crackers]

Coconut oil

Avocado oil, 2 cups

[greasing pans, spinach dip]

Artichoke hearts, 1-2 cups

[Spinach dip]

Other

1 egg

[Spinach-artichoke dip. If egg-free, use 1 cup egg-free mayo]

2-3 cups Parmesan Cheese, optional

[Spinach-artichoke dip]

Cozy Winter Suppers - Recipes and Instructions

This afternoon we are going to transform the kitchen into a production room for cozy comfort food, with plenty of veggies, and hearty protein to keep us warm and nourished. I caught myself saying quite a bit during this class, 'Just try it! Even if you think you don't like mushrooms/beets/cauliflower, everyone I've served these dishes to who said they didn't like it, didn't even realize what was in it!'

We include lots of veggies here, but they are the vegetables that are seasonal in winter: Earthy carrots and beets, bright and sweet winter squash, and creamy cauliflower. Many of the recipes are adaptable as well; if you're not sure that your family will eat this many vegetables, you can simply follow the directions, but purchase less of the vegetables when you go grocery shopping. However, vegetables are warm, filling, and add micronutrient variety or our diets, I think if you plan to include 2 side dishes of vegetables with any meal, you'll be happy with the results of how you feel!

Chicken Stock

Chicken stock is added to some the Mashed Squash and Creamy Cauliflower Mash with Chives later in the day. This recipe makes enough to have a couple quarts leftover from cooking day, which you can drink salted as a protein-rich beverage, use in savory dishes, and even toss in the slow cooker with some roasted veggies or mashed squash for an 'instant' homemade soup that you'll love!

1 pound bone-in skin-on chicken

Filtered water

2 tablespoons sea salt

--> In the bottom of a stick pot on medium heat, brown chicken.

--> Once chicken is well browned (20-45 mins) add water to fill stock pot 3/4 full.

--> Simmer stock for 3-4 hours over medium-low heat

--> Allow to cool for an hour or so, then transfer stock to quart jars.

--> Chicken meat will be pretty 'spent' by this point but it can be added to ground beef in taco meat, or added to chicken salad.

Orange-Vanilla Gummies

Feel free to use pre-made orange juice or even orange juice from concentrate (no added sugar, not fortified, no added calcium) to make these. I use fresh oranges because my children love juicing oranges, and it's something they can do to help/keeps them busy. Depending on your tastes, the honey can be reduced to 1/4 cup if desired.

3 cups orange juice, the juice from about 10 oranges

1/2 cup honey

1 cup gelatin, use Great Lakes or Perfect Supplements brand, NOT COLLAGEN

1 teaspoon vanilla (optional) *watch for added sugar*

--> Juice oranges until you get to 3 cups

--> Using a fork or whisk, whisk together orange juice and gelatin, stirring briskly as you add the gelatin to prevent clumping. Add honey and vanilla.

--> Allow to sit for 5 minutes (move on to the squash while you do this) off the heat, so the gelatin can absorb the liquid.

--> Heat over medium-low to medium heat for 10 minutes, or until liquid again.

--> Remove from heat, allow to cool until close to room temp (about 45 min)

--> Place in the fridge. To save dishes, you can place the saucepan that you mixed and cooked the gummies right in the fridge. You can also pour the mixture into candy molds to make shaped gummies. Chill for 3 hours, or until firm.

--> Run a table knife between the gummies and the saucepan, and pull out the whole gummie batch. Cut into one-inch squares or your desired shapes.

Salt and Pepper Mashed Squash

Butternut squash is my favorite to use for this, but acorn or any hard winter squash works just as well. Kobacha is our favorite squash to eat, but it usually has less flesh that is edible and more seeds and pulp, so will yield less mashed squash.

If you leave out the black pepper and garlic (just take some squash out before adding, and note on your bag) you can use this mashed squash in place of canned pumpkin in recipes. Otherwise, the pepper and garlic dress up this warm side dish.

6-12 large hard winter squash (6 butternut, 12 kobacha or acorn)

2 cloves garlic, crushed

1 teaspoon sea salt

1/2 teaspoon ground black pepper

2 tablespoons butter or coconut oil

--> Puncture squash with a sharp knife or fork in 4-5 places.

--> Bake on a baking dish or oven rack, whole, for 60 minutes at 350 degrees.

--> Allow to cool until comfortable to the touch.

--> Gently cut in half and use a large spoon to scoop out pulp, and then scoop flesh (the good part to eat) into another bowl.

--> Add garlic, sea salt, black pepper, and coconut oil to squash.

--> Place the amount of squash you will serve at one time in a quart zip-top bag, press out any air, seal, and then lay flat to freeze. Be sure to label contents and quantity on your freezer bag.

Sesame Sunflower Seed Grain Free Crackers

We rotate the sunflower seed crackers through the oven as the winter squash cooks. These crackers are delicious, and great for scooping up Spinach Artichoke Dip. Allergy-friendly, these are paleo crackers that are allowed in nut-free school lunches.

Ingredients:

1 cup unsalted sunflower seeds, hulled

1 cup sesame seeds, hulled

2 cloves garlic

Up to ¼ cup water

1 teaspoon sea salt

--> In the bowl of the food processor, using the regular metal blade, combine the sunflower seeds, salt, and garlic. Turn food processor on and let it whir for 2-3 minutes until the seeds have turned into a dense flour. Add in the sesame seeds and pulse to mix (the sesame seeds don't need to mix all the way in). Slowly add in the water, a couple tablespoons at a time, until the seeds all clump together in a ball. Remove and knead to distribute the sesame seeds through the sunflower seed mixture. The mixture isn't a very pretty color at this point, but it improves beautifully with baking.

--> Between parchment paper, roll the dough out until it is ¼ inch thick, in as close to a rectangle shape as possible. Using the parchment paper, flip the whole rectangle of dough onto a cookie sheet. Cut into rectangles with a pizza cutter or sharp knife. We'll use the cut lines to break the crackers on after they're cooked.

--> Bake at 350 degrees for 10-20 minutes, depending on thickness. Allow to cool while still on the cookie sheet, then break along scored lines and serve.

Sage Bacon-Wrapped Meatloaf

4 pounds ground beef

1-2 pounds ground pork

3 teaspoons sea salt

2 teaspoon ground black pepper

1 medium onion, finely chopped

8-12 ounces white button mushrooms, shredded or finely chopped

1 teaspoon cayenne

2 teaspoon dried sage

6 cloves garlic, crushed

2 lbs pound bacon

--> Shred the onion and mushrooms in the food processor bowl, using a slicing or grating blade. In a large bowl, combine the vegetables, and spices.

--> Once we are done with the vegetables from the food processor, get out the ground meat that you are using and mix well, making sure to break-up the meat. Within the bowl, divide the meat into 4 equal sections.

--> Form meat mixture into a loaf with your hands on parchment paper, or just on a plate

--> Get out the bacon and, starting at one end of the meat loaf, tuck one end of the bacon under the meat, and pull up and wrap it around the loaf and tuck into the other side.

--> Repeat with remaining bacon, overlapping each slice about 1/4 of the way over the previous slice.

--> If you are concerned that your meatloaf will fall apart on the way to the freezer, wrap in parchment paper. Then place in a gallon freezer zip-top bag, and press most of the air out, seal, and lay flat to freeze. Repeat with remaining meatloaves.

--> Remove Asian Meatballs from the oven as they are done; we are working on Asian-style mealtballs at the same time as the meatloaf.

Asian-Style Meatballs

Winter meals can feel heavy when they rely on red meat, cream sauces, and other rich foods. These Asian-Style Meatballs get warmth from the ginger, and deep flavor with the fish sauce and coconut aminos for a warming meal, with a lighter meat and flavor.

3 pounds ground chicken, turkey, or pork

1 bunch green onions, very thinly sliced, light green and white parts only

1/4 cup coconut aminos

2 tablespoons sesame oil

1 tablespoon fish sauce

1/2 inch fresh grated ginger

1 tablespoon sea salt

Coconut oil or avocado oil to grease pan

--> Using the chopping blade (the regular blade) in the food processor, mince onions and ginger. Place into a large mixing bowl.

--> Add coconut aminos, sesame oil, fish oil, and sea salt to the onions and ginger. Set aside until we are done working with the food processor with vegetables, and add meat when we have raw meat out for the meatloaf as well. This helps save cleanup time.

--> Add ground meat and mix in with your hands, kneading as you would bread dough to evenly distribute.

Onions and Mushrooms

While the slicing blade is in the food processor, and we're doing onions and mushrooms for the Meatloaf and Meatballs already, we will slice up some onions and mushrooms to caramelize. Add to simple baked chicken, quiche, or soup and elevate it to gourmet!

4 ounces mushrooms (the rest from the meatloaf)

3-4 large onions

1/4 teaspoon sea salt

2 tablespoons coconut oil or butter

--> Using the slicing blade on the food processor, slice onions and mushrooms

--> Sautee in a large skillet over medium heat in the coconut oil, salting to taste. Cook until onions are translucent and starting to caramelize, about 20 minutes.

Continue with...

--> Add meat to Asian-Style meatballs, roll into meatballs

--> Remove squash once it becomes soft. Allow to cool.

--> Simmer chicken stock

--> Sautee onions and mushrooms

--> Baking crackers

Roasted Root Veg & Beet Kvass

Use vegetables to taste and desire. Carrots are well-liked by most, and are simple to prepare (no peeling!). If you think that you don't like beets, try this in a small dish with just one beet to give it a try, I've had many people love beets roasted when they didn't like them any other way.

1 bunch beets*

5 lbs carrots

1 lb radishes

Avocado oil

Sea salt

--> Peel beets, scrub carrots, and remove tops from radishes.

--> Cut into bite-sized pieces*, and place in a baking dish. Drizzle with avocado oil and sprinkle with sea salt.

*--> As you are cutting up the beets, fill one quart jar 1/4 to 1/2 full with bite-sized pieces of beets. This is for your **Beet Kvass**. Add 1 tablespoon sea salt and fill to within 1 inch of top with filtered water. Cover with a air-tight (canning lid is fine) lid and let sit out to culture for 3-5 days.

--> As the last batch of crackers is done, re-use the baking sheet and oven for the Asian-Style Meatballs.

--> Continue with root vegetables after the meatballs are in the oven.

Brazilian Chicken Bites

Delicious, flavorful, and full of warming and health-giving spices, we cover bite-sized chicken thigh pieces in Brazilian flavor for quick meals.

1 tablespoon cumin

1 tablespoon coriander

1 tablespoon turmeric

1 tablespoon paprika

1/2 teaspoon cayenne pepper (omit if you want to avoid spicy)

1 teaspoon sea salt

1 teaspoon freshly ground black pepper

5 lbs boneless chicken thigh meat

--> Mix seasonings in a mixing bowl

--> Cut chicken, 1-2 lbs at a time, into approx. 1.5 inch cubes. Press into spice mixture and then place into quart zip-top bags, the desired amount in each bag (1.5 lbs is good for an average family of 4)

--> Freeze Flat.

Continue with...

--> Rinse mushrooms for meatloaf

--> Continue baking crackers.

--> Once chicken browns, add water to fill pot 1/2-3/4 full.

--> Stir gummies, mixture can be removed from heat once it is completely liquid again with no clumps.

--> Meatballs

--> Meatloaf

Cauliflower Mash with Chives

Even those who normally don't love cauliflower love this mashed cauliflower! A lighter (lower carb!) version of mashed potatoes, but with all the butter and chives that you love. Add sour cream or full fat yogurt if you tolerate dairy.

4-6 lbs Cauliflower florets (from about 2-3 heads, as much as will fit in your stock pot)

Filtered water

1 tablespoon sea salt

1/4 cup butter, ghee, or coconut oil

1 tablespoon dried chives or 1/4 cup fresh chives, diced

--> Fill stock pot with 2-3 inches filtered water. Bring to a boil over med-high heat.

--> Add cauliflower florets and cover. Allow to come to a boil again and then turn down to med-low heat to continue steaming, with the cover still on. Steam until the cauliflower is soft enough to squash with a fork, about 20 minutes.

--> Remove from heat, carefully hold lid askew and drain out most of the water used to steam.

Sauerkraut

1 head cabbage, green or purple

3 tablespoons sea salt, course is fine

2 quart sized large mouth mason jars

--> Remove and discard outer leaves of the cabbage, until you get to the clean unblemished leaves underneath. Cut cabbage in half and core.

--> Shred cabbage in food processor using a 'slicing' disk or with a knife, creating thin strips of cabbage

--> Sprinkle cabbage with 1 tablespoon sea salt. Allow to sit out for an hour, until the cabbage wilts.

-->Pack into jars, and add 1 tablespoon salt to each jar. Cover and shake to distribute the salt. . Smash to release juices.

--> Cover again, and allow to ferment on counter for 3 days before transferring to the fridge to store. Sauerkraut is ready to eat after the countertop fermentation.

Garlic-Spinach Artichoke Dip

1 cup mayonnaise

6 cups fresh spinach

2 cloves garlic

1-2 cup artichoke hearts

2-3 cups Parmesan, grated (optional)

--> Make mayonnaise

1 egg, at room temp

1 cup avocado oil

--> In a food processor, whir egg for 10-20 seconds. Then slowly add in avocado oil, taking one full minute to add. Oil will have emulsified by the time the minute is up.

--> Add in fresh spinach, filling the food processor full, whirring until mixed in, and then repeating the process with the reamining spinach.

--> Add artichoke hearts and pulse to chop.

--> Mix in the cheese if using and enjoy!

Serve with crackers or fresh vegetables.

Cozy Winter Suppers Storage and Reheating Instructions

Bacon-Wrapped Meatloaf

To store: Freeze flat in a zip-top bag, wrapping in parchment paper or freezer paper if desired.

Use within: 6 months.

Reheat: Thaw overnight in the fridge, on a 8x8 or similarly sized baking dish. Once thawed, bake at 375*, uncovered, for 55 minutes or until reaches an internal temperature of 160* F.

Serving suggestions: Delicious with Mashed Squash or Cauliflower Mash.

Asian-Style Meatballs

To Store: Allow to cool, freeze in a gallon zip-top freezer bag, be careful not to squish while freezing. Once frozen, it's easy to remove as many meatballs as you need at one time.

Use within: 6 months.

Reheat: Thaw 8-12 hours in the fridge. From thawed, melt a tablespoon of fat (butter, coconut oil, bacon grease, etc) in a large skillet and sauté over medium heat for 10-12 minutes or until cooked through.

Serving Suggestions: Add some zoodles (zucchini noodles) or any frozen vegetable (I like broccoli too) to the skillet as you sauté for a quick one-pan dinner. Make a reduction sauce (recipe follows) to serve with.

Reduction Sauce:

1 tablespoon apple cider vinegar

2 cups broth

1/2 teaspoon sea salt

1/2 teaspoon ginger, garlic, black pepper, or seasoning of choice

2-3 tablespoons honey

Keep the shallow pan used to pan-fry meat over medium heat and add apple cider vinegar and water or 1/4 cup of the bone broth. Use a fork or whisk to whisk deglaze the pan, lifting up all the flavorful burnt on bits. Add the broth cubes or remainder of the broth, sea salt, seasonings, and honey and reduce heat to a simmer. Simmer the sauce while whisking occasionally for 10 minutes, or until reduced by half.

Sunflower Seed Crackers

To Store: Freeze in zip-top bags or plastic containers, laying flat to freeze and being careful not to crush.

Use within: 4 months.

Reheat: Not necessary, these thaw quickly!

Serving Suggestions: Use to dip any dip of choice, top with cheese or sliced meat, top with salmon, chicken, or egg salad.

Brazilian Chicken Bites

To Store: Place seasoned, raw chicken in quart zip-top bag and press out air. Allow to freeze flat.

Use within: 6 months.

Reheat: Thaw 8-12 hours in the fridge, or 1 hour on counter. From thawed or partially thawed, melt a tablespoon of fat (butter, coconut oil, bacon grease, etc) in a large skillet and sauté over medium heat for 15-20 minutes or until cooked through.

Serving Suggestions: Delicious with cauliflower rice and topped with coconut milk as a dressing or dip.

Orange Juice Gummies

To Store: Freeze flat in zip-top bags or keep covered in the fridge.

Use within:6 Months frozen, 1 week in the refrigerator.

Reheat: Thaw overnight in the fridge.

Serving Suggestions: Use as a treat or a snack.

Sauerkraut

To Store: After initial fermentation, 'burp' your ferment (unscrew lid, and allow excess air to escape- do this over the sink) and then store in the fridge.

Use within: Once you start using a ferment, you introduce bacteria every time you open the jar, so try to use the jar within 10 days of first use. Otherwise, unopened (after the initial 'burping') ferments will stay in the fridge for 6 months or longer.

Reheat: Keep raw to keep enzymes and probiotics intact.

Serving Suggestions: Serve alongside all meals as a condiment to provide needed probiotics. You may be surprised- children often LOVE ferments!

Beet Kvass

To Store: After initial fermentation, 'burp' your ferment (unscrew lid, and allow excess air to escape- do this over the sink) and then store in the fridge.

Use within: Once you start using a ferment, you introduce bacteria every time you open the jar, so try to use the jar within 10 days of first use. Otherwise, unopened (after the initial 'burping') ferments will stay in the fridge for 6 months or longer.

Reheat: Keep raw to keep enzymes and probiotics intact.

Serving Suggestions: Drink 1-2 ounces in the morning as a digestive tonic. Combine with oil (fresh pressed olive oil is great!) as a salad dressing.

Roasted Vegetables

To Store: Freeze in zip-top bags or plastic containers, laying flat to freeze and being careful not to crush.

Use within: 4 months.

Reheat: Thaw overnight in the fridge if desired, or on the counter for an hour. Can be heated from frozen, simply increase the cooking time by 5-10 minutes.

Cook in a skillet with a little fat over medium heat, covered for the first 10 minutes and then uncovered.

Serving Suggestions:

Add to soups: Fill a slow cooker 1/2 full with frozen roasted vegetables. Add 1 quart of chicken stock, and fill with filtered water until the slow cooker is 3/4 full. Cook on low 8-10 hours, add some chopped cooked meat at the end.

Stovetop soup directions: Fill a sauce pan 1/2 full with frozen roasted vegetables. Add 1-2 cups chicken stock, and fill with filtered water until sauce pan is 3/4 full. Heat over medium-

These can eaten cold or room temperature as well, drizzle with salad dressing of choice.

Mashed Winter Squash

To Store: Freeze in zip-top bags or plastic containers, laying flat to freeze and being careful not to crush.

Use within: 4 months.

Reheat: Thaw overnight in the fridge if desired, or on the counter for an hour. Can be heated from frozen, simply increase the cooking time by 5-10 minutes.

Cook in a skillet with a little fat over medium heat, covered for the first 10 minutes and then uncovered until heated through and excess liquid has evaporated. .

Serving Suggestions:

Serve as a side dish.

Creamy Cauliflower-Chive Mash

To Store: Freeze in zip-top bags or plastic containers, laying flat to freeze and being careful not to crush.

Use within: 4 months.

Reheat: Thaw overnight in the fridge if desired, or on the counter for an hour. Can be heated from frozen, simply increase the cooking time by 5-10 minutes.

Cook in a skillet with a little fat over medium heat, covered for the first 10 minutes and then uncovered until heated through. Can also be baked alongside another dish (ie if you're making a roast) for 45 minutes. Cover during baking.

Serving Suggestions:

Add to soups: Fill a slow cooker 1/2 full with frozen roasted vegetables. Add 1 quart of chicken stock, and fill with filtered water until the slow cooker is 3/4 full. Cook on low 8-10 hours, add some chopped cooked meat at the end.

Onions and Mushrooms

To Store: Freeze in zip-top bags or plastic containers, laying flat to freeze and being careful not to crush.

Use within: 4 months.

Reheat: Thaw overnight in the fridge if desired, or on the counter for an hour. Can be heated from frozen, simply increase the cooking time by 5-10 minutes.

Cook in a skillet with a little fat over medium heat, covered for the first 10 minutes and then uncovered.

Serving Suggestions:

Add to soups, quiche, as a side dish with chicken, beef, lamb, etc.

Chicken Stock

To Store: If you aren't using within 1 week, add 1 tablespoon sea salt per quart of chicken stock (just add it into the jar and shake a bit). Store in the fridge, covered. Quart mason jars work well for this.

Use within: 3 weeks.

Reheat: Simmer in a sauce pan.

Serving Suggestions:

Add to soups as directed, replace 1/2 the water in any savory dish (rice, etc) with chicken stock.

Spinach-Artichoke Dip

To Store: Store in the fridge, covered.

Use within: 10 days.

Reheat: Not needed

Serving Suggestions:

Use to top soups, serve with Asian-style meatballs, dip carrot slices or cucumber slices in it, eat with Sunflower Crackers.

Warm Weather Favorites - Overview and Grocery List

Cooking Day Overview

Recipes made:

Chicken Enchilada Casserole (4 meals that serve 4 each)

Cabbage-Apple Salad (3-4)

Cut up Watermelon (1 watermelon)

Chicken Pepper Bacon Bites (4-6)

Lemon-Pepper Chicken (2-3)

Yogurt (12 servings)

Strawberry Chia Jam (1 pint)

Strawberry-Lemonade Gummie Treats (8 servings)

Sunflower Crackers (4 meals)

Cooked Steak Slices (4-6 meals)

Kimchi (2 quarts)

Bananas (enough for 6+ smoothie batches)

Banana Coconut-Flour Muffins, (2 doz)

Equipment Used:

Yogurt or kefir for smoothies, yogurt dressing : *Stock Pot*

Enchilada Sauce: *Large Sauce Pan*

Basic: Salt and Pepper Sunflower Crackers *Food Processor, baking sheet*

Strawberry Chia Jam *Blender/Jar*

Strawberry-Lemonade Gummies *Blender/Small Sauce Pan*

Cabbage-Apple Slaw with Yogurt Dressing *Cutting Board*

Kimchi *Cutting Board/Food Processor*

Chicken Pepper Bacon Bites *Cutting board*

Lemon Pepper Chicken for meals, chicken salad, chicken stock *Cutting Board, Large baking sheet*

Steak *Griddle or Grill*

Spaghetti Squash

Easy Cut-Up Watermelon

Freeze Bananas for Smoothies

Yogurt	Stockpot	Heat over med heat
Spaghetti Squash	Enchilada Casseroles	Puncture and Bake
Sunflower seeds	Crackers/oven	Make dough, roll, and bake
Cleanup	Check Yogurt	Keep Baking crackers
Enchilada Sauce	Peel Bananas for Smoothies	Remove yogurt from heat
Puree strawberries	Strawberry Gummies	Chia Jam
Slice Cabbage	Cabbage-apple Salad	Kimchi
Kimchi	Heat Gummies	Continue Simmering Enchilada Sauce
Remove Spaghetti Squash	Crackers are done, turn off oven	Contine Kimchi
Kimchi Cont.		
Heat griddle to med-high for steak	Heat oven to 350 for lemon-pepper chicken	Prep steak and chicken
Chicken Pepper Poppers	Turn steak	Once milk is cool enough that it is ok to touch, do yogurt.
Yogurt	Prepare Spaghetti Squash	Pepper poppers are still in progress
Assemble Enchilada Casseroles	Finish pepper poppers and clip ends	
Cut watermelon		
Make Muffins		
		You're done! :)

Grocery List

Meat

Steak, any kind, 4-6 lbs

Chicken, thighs, skin-on, bone-in, 4 lbs

[Lemon pepper Chicken]

Chicken, boneless skinless, 5 lbs

[Chicken Bacon Bites 2 lbs]

[Enchilada Spaghetti Squash Casserole 3 lbs]

Bacon, 2 lbs (*watch for added sugar*)

[Chicken Bacon Bites]

Produce

Spaghetti Squash, 4 medium

[Enchilada Casserole]

Onion,

[Enchilada Sauce, 1 large]

Strawberries, 3 lbs

[Strawberry-Lemonade Gummies]

[Strawberry-Chia Jam]

Lemons, 8

*Can use bottled lemon juice

[Gummies – 5]

[Chia Jam – 1]

[Chicken pepper bites – 1]

Bananas, 2-3 bunches

* GAPS or SCD: They need to be ripe, with spots.

[For Smoothies]

[4 for Muffins]

Cabbage, 1 head

[Cabbage-Apple Salad]

[Kimchi]

Cabbage, Napa, 1 head

Carrots, 1 pound

Radishes, 1 bunch

Garlic, 1 head

Chili, Anaheim, 6

Watermelon, 1

Green onions, 1 bunch

Ginger root, 1

Seasonings

Sea salt *(You will use more of this than you expect- buy at least 1/2 cup, if you find it in bulk bins there is usually substantial savigs by buying it there)*

Black pepper

Cayenne

Paprika

Oregano

Cumin

Lemon-pepper seasoning *(watch for added sugar)*

Pantry Items

Honey, 1 pint

4 cups sunflower seeds, hulled, unsalted

2 cups sesame seeds

Tomato paste, 18 ounces

Lemon Juice (as a sub for fresh lemon juice)

Coconut flour, 1-1/2 cups

[muffins]

Walnuts, 2 cups, optional

[muffins]

Chia seeds, 1/4 cup

Other*

Milk, whole, 1 gallon

Cream or half an half, 1 quart

1/4 cup plain yogurt to start your culture

[Yogurt]

Wooden Skewers for Chicken Bacon Bites

Notes:

Warm Weather Favorites - Instructions and Recipes

24-hour Yogurt

If Dairy Free, make coconut yogurt as directed on your non-dairy yogurt starter.

Commercial yogurt is not allowed as it has not been incubated long enough to use up all the lactose. The 24-hour incubation at 100 degrees Fahrenheit gives the culture sufficient time to use up the vast majority of the lactose, making yogurt acceptable on the diet.

Ingredients:

1 gallon Milk + 1 quart heavy cream (goat or cow, raw or pasteurized. Preferably raw and from cows or goats eating fresh pasture)

Yogurt starter (The Specific Carbohydrate Diet requires a yogurt starter with only acidophilus. On the GAPS diet plain high quality yogurt from the health food store can be used as the starter. See Grocery List for recommendations.)

Directions:

In a stock pot, heat milk gently on medium heat, stirring approximately every 10 minutes, until milk is close to a boil.

Cover, remove from burner, and allow to cool until the yogurt is comfortable to the touch, 90-110 degrees Fahrenheit.

Make sure the yogurt is not too hot at this stage, or you will kill the good bacteria that are going to make your milk into yogurt.

Pour nearly warm milk into clean quart jars.

Using one tablespoon of commercial yogurt per quart, (or follow the directions that came with your powdered starter) mix yogurt or starter into the jars of warm milk.

Cover and shake to distribute culture.

Keep warm in a yogurt maker, Excalibur dehydrator or cooler at 100 degrees for a full 24 hours. Yogurt is now done and should be kept in the refrigerator.

Spaghetti Squash Enchilada Bowls

These spaghetti squash enchilada bowls are simple to put together - the squash halves roast as you are whipping up the enchilada sauce and cooking the chicken. They are delicious too- with the slightly sweet taste and delicate texture of the spaghetti squash complementing the spicy-smokey enchilada sauce and hearty chicken.

Serving Suggestion: *Any Mexican-style topping works well with this dish, you can see cheese, sliced black olives, and sliced green onions here. Guacamole, sour cream, or fermented salsa would be great toppings as well.*

Ingredients:

4 medium spaghetti squash

2 tablespoon coconut oil

2 pound boneless chicken thighs or breasts

18 oz tomato paste

3 teaspoon sea salt

1 teaspoon cayenne

1 teaspoon cumin

2 teaspoon smoked paprika

2 teaspoon dried oregano

1 onion, diced

4 cups chicken stock

---> Preheat oven to 350*.

---> Puncture spaghetti squash and bake for 1 hour, or until soft when pushed firmly.

Allow to cool, cut, and scoop out pulp. Set aside spaghetti strands for casserole.

---> Make the enchilada sauce by mixing the tomato paste, spices, and onion in a small saucepan with a fork. Gradually add chicken stock to thin the mixture.

Once the chicken has been browned, reduce heat to medium-low and add the enchilada sauce. Cover. Allow to simmer, covered, stirring every 10 minutes or so, until the squash is done.

Once the squash is done, remove from heat and allow it to cool for 5 minutes. Remove the chicken-enchilada sauce mixture from the heat as well.

Use a fork to separate all the spaghetti strings of each squash half, leaving the squash in the bowl for serving. Top with the chicken enchilada mixture and toppings of choice. Enjoy hot!

Sesame Sunflower Seed Grain Free Crackers

Ingredients:

4 cups unsalted sunflower seeds, hulled

Up to 1/2 cup water

1 tablespoon sea salt (the coarse kind is fine)

Extra salt, pepper, and other seasonings of choice for sprinkling.

Directions:

--> Oven is already at 350* for the spaghetti squash.

--> In the bowl of the food processor, using the regular metal blade, combine the sunflower seeds, salt, and garlic. Turn food processor on and let it whir for 2-3 minutes until the seeds have turned into a dense flour. . Slowly add in the water, a couple tablespoons at a time, until the seeds all clump together in a ball. Remove and knead to distribute the sesame seeds through the sunflower seed mixture. The mixture isn't a very pretty color at this point, but it improves beautifully with baking.

---> Between parchment paper, roll the dough out until it is 1/8 inch thick, in as close to a rectangle shape as possible. Using the parchment paper, flip the whole rectangle of dough onto a cookie sheet. Cut into rectangles with a pizza cutter or sharp knife. We'll use the cut lines to break the crackers on after they're cooked.

--> Bake at 350 degrees for 10-20 minutes, depending on thickness. Allow to cool while still on the cookie sheet, then break along scored lines and serve.

---> Continue to roll out the remaining cracker dough, using fresh parchment under each batch; we will rotate these crackers through the oven for the next hour or so.

--> Make Enchilada Sauce for Spaghetti Squash Casserole.

Strawberry Lemonade Gummies

Ingredients:

2 cups strawberry puree

1/2 cup lemon juice (from about 5 lemons)

4+ tablespoons raw honey

1 cup gelatin

Directions:

---> Puree 3 lbs of strawberries

---> Add 4 tablespoons honey (to taste)

---> Place half the mixture in a saucepan

Combine all ingredients except gelatin. Add gelatin and use a whisk or immersion blender to thoroughly combine fruit and gelatin.

--> Allow gelatin to absorb liquid for 5 minutes. Then heat over medium heat until gelatin all melts.

Pour mixture into silicone candy molds or an 8×8-inch glass baking dish. Cover tightly and chill for 1 hour or longer.

Remove pan or molds from refrigerator and remove gummies. If using a baking dish, use a spatula to gently loosen the edges and part of the bottom of the gelatin from the sides of the dish. Gently turn it upside down onto a cutting board and let the gelatin fall out. Use a large knife to cut it into squares or strips. Refrigerate any leftovers.

Chia Seed Jam

1 pound berries

¼ cup honey

2 tablespoons chia seeds

1 tablespoon lemon juice

--> The berries have already been pureed and are in the blender.

--> Add in lemon juice and chia seeds and mix. Place in a pint mason jar, and allow to sit in the fridge for 4 hours, or longer, as the chia seeds absorb the liquid. ---

---> Use as regular jam, keeping in the fridge.

Cabbage-Apple Salad

3/4 head cabbage (the rest will be used for kimchi)

2 medium apples

--> Continue with crackers

Kimchi

Approx 3 cups cabbage (from cabbage-apple salad)

1 pound carrots

1 Anaheim chili

1 bunch green onions

1 bunch radishes

1 head napa cabbage

1 inch ginger, minced

4 cloves garlic, minced

3 tablespoons sea salt

--> Use the slicing blade, slice all ingredients.

--> Add the remaining cabbage left from the cabbage-apple salad.

---> Cover with sea salt, toss to mix. Let sit out 20 minutes or until wilted.

--> Pack into jars, covering with filtered water if needed.

Cooked Steak

We cook whatever steaks you have on hand (I like to find what's on discount at the store because it is closer to expiring.) Use for fast protein; Sliced on crackers, in sandwiches, over salads, or just to eat on its own.

4 steaks, any kind

Salt and pepper, to taste

--> Heat griddle over medium-high heat. Sear steak for 5 minutes, and then flip. Once you flip, turn down to medium-low and continue cooking until cooked through, about 10-15 more minutes depending on thickness of the steak.

Lemon-Pepper Chicken

This flavorful chicken is baked in the oven and easy for those meals when you need protein, but don't want to heat up the house. Enjoy for lunches and dinners!

4 lbs Bone-in Skin-on Chicken Thighs

1 teaspoon sea salt

1 tablespoon lemon-pepper

Preheat oven to 375*

--> Lay chicken, skin side up, in a shallow baking dish. Sprinkle with salt and pepper.

---> Bake for 25 minutes, or until cooked through.

Keep in the fridge or freezer, covered.

Chicken Pepper Bacon Bites

2-3 lbs boneless/skinless chicken

1 lemon, juiced

1 teaspoon lemon-pepper seasoning

--> Marinade

4-5 Anaheim Chilies

2 lbs bacon

Cut the marinaded chicken in bite-sized pieces.

Cut tops off chilies, slit down one side (lengthwise) and rinse out seeds. Cut into bite-sized pieces.

Cut bacon in half lengthwise.

Wrap chicken in pepper piece, then in bacon, then secure on skewer. Fit 4-5 on each skewer and then repeat until remaining ingredients are used up.

Everything is coming together!

---> Yogurt should be cool enough to place in jars and incubate.

---> Start preparing spaghetti squash: Grease pans, scoop out seeds and pulp from the centers of the squash. Use a fork to tease into spaghetti strands and press evenly into 3 or 4 greased pans.

--> Lemon Pepper Chicken will be done soon. Remove from oven and allow to cool before transferring to a lidded container or zip-top bag.

--> As steak finishes cooking, chicken for enchilada casserole will be grilled.

--> Distribute enchilada sauce evenly over spaghetti squash. Cube and add chicken once grilled.

--> Continue with chicken pepper bites. Use wire clippers to trim wood skewers to fit in zip-top bag (and not poke through!) once done.

Cut Watermelon

Quick snacks and as a dessert treat, pre-cut watermelon is easy to eat straight from the fridge.

Still have energy?

Coconut Flour Banana Muffins

Makes 2 dozen

2 tablespoons coconut oil+ another tablespoon to grease the pan

4 ripe bananas
1/2 cup honey
6 eggs
1/2 cup full fat coconut milk
1-1/2 cup coconut flour
2 lemons, juiced
1 teaspoon vanilla
1/2 teaspoon sea salt
1 teaspoon baking soda

2 cups walnuts, optional

Directions

Preheat oven to 375* F.

Line 2 muffin pans with parchment muffin liners. Dot muffin liners with the one tablespoon of coconut oil, and allow coconut oil to melt in the oven.

In a stand mixer, bowl, or food processor mash or puree the bananas and combine them with the eggs, remaining coconut oil, yogurt or coconut milk, coconut flour, lemon juice, vanilla, and sea salt.

After the mixture is smooth, add in the baking soda and mix again.

Fill prepared muffin tin with batter, filling ¾ full.

Bake for 35 minutes or until a knife inserted in the middle of the largest muffin comes out clean.

Warm Weather Favorites - Storage and Reheating Instructions

Yogurt

To store: After incubating in the dehydrator for 24 hours, move to fridge.

Use within:6 weeks.

Tips: Yogurt will firm up in the fridge.

Serving suggestions: Add dried fruit, chopped nuts, flaked coconut, or chia jam to yogurt cups.

Spaghetti Squash Enchilada Casserole

To Store: Cover tightly with foil. Slip into a freezer bag.

Use within: 6 months.

Reheat: Thaw all day in the fridge. Keep covered, and heat at 375* for 45 minutes, and then uncover for an additional 15-20 minutes, or until heated through.

Serving Suggestions: Top with sliced green onions, yogurt (or sour cream), sliced olives, salsa, or guacamole.

Sunflower Seed Crackers

To Store: Freeze in zip-top bags or plastic containers, laying flat to freeze and being careful not to crush.

Use within: 4 months.

Reheat: Not necessary, these thaw quickly!

Serving Suggestions: Use to dip any dip of choice, top with cheese or sliced meat, top with salmon, chicken, or egg salad.

Strawberry Chia Jam

To Store: Keep covered in the refrigerator.

Use within: 10 days.

Reheat: Not needed, though it can be heated for a pancake topping.

Notes: If it doesn't thicken in the fridge overnight to regular jam consistency, add another tablespoon of chia seeds, and stir. Some fruit has higher water content than others, and more chia is needed.

Strawberry-Lemonade Gummies

To Store: Freeze flat in zip-top bags or keep covered in the fridge.

Use within:6 Months frozen, 1 week in the refridgerator.

Reheat: Thaw overnight in the fridge.

Serving Suggestions: Use as a treat or a snack.

Cabbage-Apple Slaw

To Store: Keep covered in the fridge.

Use within: 5 days, when combined with dressing below.

Reheat: Not needed.

Serving Suggestions: Top with yogurt dressing- whisk together:

- 1/2 cup yogurt (dairy or non dairy)
- 1 tablespoon apple cider vinegar
- 1 tablespoon minced fresh ginger or 1/2 teaspoon dried
- 1 teaspoon coarse sea salt

Lemon-Pepper Chicken

To Store: Freeze flat in zip-top bags. Or keep covered in the fridge.

Use within:6 Months frozen, 1 week in the fridge.

Reheat: Thaw overnight in the fridge. Dish will still be partially frozen in the morning. To heat, place on a baking dish and heat at 375* for 20 minutes, or until hot. Or enjoy cold from the fridge.

Serving Suggestions: Served with a cheese slice or handful of nuts and sliced fruit, this is a fast meal for days that you can't stand heating up the kitchen!

Kimchi

To Store: After initial fermentation, 'burp' your ferment (unscrew lid, and allow excess air to escape- do this over the sink) and then store in the fridge.

Use within: Once you start using a ferment, you introduce bacteria every time you open the jar, so try to use the jar within 10 days of first use. Otherwise, unopened (after the initial 'burping') ferments will stay in the fridge for 6 months or longer.

Reheat: Keep raw to keep enzymes and probiotics intact.

Serving Suggestions: Serve alongside all meals as a condiment to provide needed probiotics. You may be surprised- children often LOVE ferments!

Chicken-Pepper-Bacon Bites

To Store: After snipping off the ends with wire cutters, freeze flat in zip-top bags.

Use within:3 Months.

Reheat: Pull out desired amount. Place in shallow baking dish (8x8 pan or pie plate works well). The skewers can be propped on the edge of the pan. Bake at 375* for 30 minutes or grill over indirect heat for 30 minutes, or until chicken in the center is firm and bacon is crispy.

Serving Suggestions: This is a great potluck dish!

Steak

To Store: Slice thinly across the grain with a chef's knife once cooled. Keep frozen in a zip top bag or covered in the fridge.

Use within:6 Months from the freezer, 1 week in the fridge.

Reheat: Pan fry if desired, but enjoy cold to keep everyone cool!

Serving Suggestions: Serve with crackers and fresh watermelon for a cool meal! In addition, you can cut thinly and combine with mayonnaise, mustard, and sliced pickles for a 'steak salad' (similar to chicken salad)

Frozen Bananas

To Store: Keep in a zip-top bag in the freezer. To help keep from sticking together, try to break up the bananas once partially frozen (after a couple hours).

Use within: 4 months

Reheat: Thawed, these can be used in baked goods. Otherwise use in smoothies frozen.

Serving Suggestions: Blend with your favorite smoothie ingredients!

Some sample smoothies:

Berries and Cream

2 frozen bananas

1 can coconut milk

1 cup fresh berries

1 teaspoon vanilla

Blend til smooth

Probiotic Protein Power

2 frozen bananas

2 cups milk kefir

1/4 cup peanutbutter

Up to 1 cup ice cubes

Blend bananas, milk kefir, and peanutbutter til smooth. Add ice cubes as needed if the smoothie is too rich.

Watermelon

To Store: Cover in a bowl in the fridge.

Use within:1 week.

Serving Suggestions: In addition to using this as a snack, it can be pureed in the bowl with an immersion blender, add honey to taste, and frozen in popsicle molds!

Mediterranean Meals - Overview and Grocery List

Grocery list

Meat

Ground Turkey, 4 lbs

(can also use chicken, beef, or lamb)

[Greek Burgers]

Boneless Lamb Roast (shoulder or leg), 2-3 lbs

[Lamb Shish kebabs]

Ground Beef, 8 lbs

(can also be ground pork, or a combination of both)

4 lbs [Lasagna for people who eat dairy OR Stuffed Zucchini for the dairy free version]

4 lbs [Veggie-Packed Meatballs]

Produce

Zucchini, 10 lbs

5-6 lbs [Zucchini Lasagna OR Stuffed Squash]
1 [Veggie-packed meatballs]
2 lbs [Roasted Summer Vegetables]
1 lb [Zucchini Almond Flour Muffins]

Cauliflower, 1 head/ 1-2 lbs of florettes

1 head Italian Pickled Vegetables

Bell Peppers, red, 3 ea

1 [Italian pickled vegetables]

2 [Lamb shish kebabs]

Chili Pepper (Sereno or Anaheim) 3

1 Greek Turkey Burgers

3 Italian Pickled Vegetables (can be jalapenos)

Carrots, 4

2 Veggie-Packed Meatballs

2 Italian Pickled Vegetables

Tomatoes, Cherry, 8 oz

[Roasted Summer Vegetables]

Onions, 1 yellow, 6 red

1 yellow Veggie-Packed Meatballs
3 red Greek Shish Kebabs

1 red Italian Pickled Vegetables

2 red Roasted Summer Vegetables

Lemons, 9

2 Greek Shish Kebabs

1 Greek Turkey Burgers

4 Dill-Coconut Dippng Sauce

2 Roasted Italian Vegetables

Mushrooms, 2 lbs

Roasted vegetables

Greek Shish Kebabs

Fresh Herbs

(*Dried can be substituted for all- use 1/4 the amount of dried*)

Mint (2 cups chopped- one bunch)

Oregano, 1 bunch

Basil, 2 bunchs

Thyme, 2 sprigs

Dill, 2 tablespoons (one small bunch)

Seasonings

Parsley

Oregano

Thyme

Basil

Dill

Celery seed

Dried mustard

Sea salt

Black pepper

Paprika

Garlic Powder

Onion Powder

Cinnamon

Pantry Items

Almond flour, 4 cups (zucchini muffins)

Crushed tomatoes, 2 cans- Zucchini Lasagna *OR* Tomato paste, 2 cans - Stuffed Squash - non dairy option

Coconut milk, 3 cans

Olive oil

Apple Cider Vinegar

Honey, 1 cup

Gelatin, 1 tablespoon

Vanilla

Dairy: [zucchini lasagna only]

Mozarella, 2 cups shredded

Goat cheese, dry curd cottage cheese, or regular cottage cheese, 3 cups

Parmesan, 1 cup shredded

Eggs

Eggs, 16 (Coconut Pudding, Zucchini Muffins)

Step	Recipe	Notes
Use food processor to shred veggies and dice fresh herbs	Greek Turkey Burgers Lamb Kebabs Meatballs	Just rinse between uses
Assemble fermented vegetables	Italian Pickled Vegetables	
Make Dressings	Coconut-Dill Sauce, Italian Herbed Dressing	
Marinate Lamb	Lamb Skewers	Cover and chill
Mix turkey into herb mix	Greek Turkey Burgers	Roll meatballs as these cook
Make Meatballs	Veggie-Packed Meatballs	Bake, finish grilling turkey burgers, start grilling zucchini
Slice and grill zucchini	Zucchini Lasagna OR Stuffed Zucchini	* Sliced for lasagna, halved for stuffed zucchini
Brown meat, season once browned	Zucchini Lasagna OR Stuffed Zucchini	Continue grilling zucchini
Roast Summer Vegetables		Bake zucchini dish for tonight's dinner if desired
Assemble lamb kebabs		
Make zucchini muffins	Almond-Flour Zucchini Muffins	Make pudding as they bake
Make Pudding		

Notes:

Mediterranean Meals - Instructions and Recipes

Let's Get Started

Make your Herb/veggie mixes for the Greek Lamb Burgers, Veggie-Packed Meatballs, and Greek Turkey Patties

Use your food processor to dice, shred, and chop all needed veggies, place ingredients for each in separate bowls to mix meat in after putting away the food processor.

-> It is good practice to get all the veggies done and put away before working with raw meat, so that we don't have to worry about raw meat getting into our veggies.

-> We can also pulse all the raw veggies and herbs through the food processor with just a quick rinse between uses, since the flavors all complement eachother.

Aren't these fresh herbs and veggies great to work with? So vibrant, flavorful, health-giving and aromatic!

Tip: Any extras? If you have odds and ends (not cup-fulls, that will alter the recipe, but up to 1/4 cup each) just toss them in the meatball bowl. The meatballs are just enhanced by different herbs and veggies.

Greek Shish Kebabs

-> Make Marinade:

2 tablespoons fresh oregano (about 6 stalks) or 2 teaspoons dried

1 large onion

1/3 cup olive oil

2 lemons, juiced

1/2 teaspoon sea salt

2 cloves garlic

-> Then add these Ingredients:

3 pounds lean boneless lamb or beef (leg or shoulder), trimmed of fat and cut into 1 ½-inch cubes

2 large red onion, cut into 1-inch pieces

2 large red or green pepper, cut into 1 ½-inch pieces

1/2 pound mushrooms, whole

[Greek Shish Kebabs Continued]

Directions:

Combine marinade ingredients in a gallon-sized plastic bag or in a bowl. Add lamb or beef cubes, seal bag and shake/mix contents until meat is coated in marinade. Place bag in a bowl in the refrigerator and allow meat to marinate for the rest of the cooking day. Periodically squish contents of bag around to keep all the meat well coated in marinade.

--> After marinating, carefully remove meat from the bag and drain quickly in a colander in the sink. Place the onion, pepper, and mushrooms into bag and coat them in the marinade. Remove them from the bag as well.

--> On skewers, thread the meat and vegetables alternately then place them on a lightly greased grill over medium-high heat.

To cook: Cook shish kebabs for 12-15 minutes, basting them frequently with leftover marinade until meat and vegetables are well browned and cooked to your desired doneness.

Greek Turkey Burgers

1/2 cup chopped mint

1 Sereno pepper, or Anaheim chili, finely diced

1 lemon, juiced

4 teaspoons paprika

2 cloves garlic

-> Mix above as your spice mixture.

Tip: Prone to forgetting where you are? Use a pen to mark off each ingredient as it's in your bowl

Tip: You'll know this mixture is for the turkey when we get to the step where we add the meat because of all the mint and paprika.

4 lbs ground turkey (cut with 1 lb beef if desired)

2 teaspoons sea salt

Dash black pepper

-> Mix into spice mixture during the step where we add the raw meat to the meat dishes.

Veggie-Packed Grain Free Meatballs

--> Use food processer to shred vegetables, and any fresh herbs

2-3 carrots

1 onion

1-3 zucchini or other summer squash

4 cloves garlic, crushed

[Veggie-packed meatballs continued...]

--> Later add:

4 pounds ground beef (or other ground meat- using 1 or 2 pounds of venison, pork, etc)

1 tablespoon sea salt

1/2 teaspoon freshly ground black pepper

--> Using a food processor or grater, grate the veggies, herbs, and salt and pepper.

--> Mix in with the meat, adding in salt and pepper. Form into balls (you can do this right in the same bowl you mixed the meat in to save dishes).

--> After mixing in meat, roll into 1-2 inch diameter balls, and place in a single layer on a shallow baking dish or cookie sheet with sides.

--> Preheat oven broiler to high. Broil for 8 minutes, or until tops are browning, but they are not cooked through. Meatballs will cook more once we re-heat them.

Kids can help: Roll meatballs.

--> Storage instructions: Freeze extra meatballs in a single layer on a cookie sheet. Transfer frozen meatballs to a zip top bag and return to freezer.

Tip: Following along with the outline, before we get out raw meat, we make dipping sauce and dressings and cultured vegetables

Ferment: Italian Pickled Vegetables

Nutrition tip: Serve alongside all the dinners here, to help with digestion and provide usable vitamin C and probiotics.

Ingredients:

1 head cauliflower

1 red bell pepper

1 red, white, or yellow onion

2-4 carrots

2-4 stalks celery

10 large garlic cloves

2 jalapeno or Serrano peppers

2 sprigs fresh thyme

1 teaspoon of sea salt per pint OR 1 tablespoon per quart jar

Directions: Rinse all produce. Seed and coarsely chop peppers. Peel and thinly slice onion. Slice carrot thinly, cut cauliflower into florets. Fill quart mason jars even with all vegetables, garlic, and thyme. Add filtered water to cover vegetables, and top with 1 tablespoon unrefined sea salt. Screw on Mason jar lids to finger-tight and allow to culture on the counter away from light for 5 days. Transfer to the fridge.

Dill-Coconut Dipping Sauce

1 can coconut milk

4 lemons, juiced

2 teaspoons dried dill OR 2 tablespoons fresh, snipped with scissors

2 tablespoons crushed garlic

1 teaspoon parsley, dried

1.5 teaspoon sea salt

[Dill-Coconut Dipping Sauce Continued...]

Instructions: Mix all ingredients. Freeze in approx 1/3 cup portions (makes 4)

Italian Dressing

Tip: When you have healthy dressing on hand, it's easy to just toss with some fresh salad greens, and whatever veggies you have on hand for a healthy delicious salad or over grilled, roasted, or sautéed summer squash.

Ingredients:

2/3 cup extra virgin olive oil

1/4 cup apple cider vinegar

1 tsp. raw honey, melted

1 1/2 tsp. dried oregano

1/4 tsp. dried thyme

1/4 tsp. dried basil

1/4 tsp. dried parsley

1 tsp. garlic powder

1 tsp. onion powder

1/8 tsp. celery seed

1/4 tsp. dried mustard

1 1/2 tsp. sea salt

1/4 tsp. ground black pepper

Combine in a mason jar, and gently swirl to mix before using.

--> Go back and add the lamb to your marinade, beef and/or pork to your veggies from the meatballs, and turkey to the mint/paprika mixture in the bowls.

--> Cover lamb, chill and allow the marinade to be absorbed.

--> Start grilling Greek Turkey Burgers- We want to cook them so they aren't quite done (they will continue to cook while reheating) so try for just 5-7 minutes on each side.

--> Roll meatballs as the turkey burgers cook, place in a single layer on a cookie sheet with sides and/or shallow baking dishes, and bake.

Kids Help! Have kids that need a job? If they can roll play-dough balls, they can roll meatballs! Set them up near you and check every so often to ensure the meatballs are similar size, but otherwise let them be in charge of this process.

--> Start on zucchini lasagna and/or zucchini boats

--> Brown meat mixture

--> Slice and grill zucchini slices for lasagna OR

--> Halve and start grilling halves for stuffed zucchini

---> Add seasonings to meat mixture, assemble lasagna or stuffed zucchini as directed.

Zucchini Lasagna**

Allergy Tip: This recipe has dairy- for those avoiding dairy, see the next recipe, Sausage-Stuffed Zucchini Boats

Ingredients:

5-6 pounds zucchini, sliced thinly lengthwise to make "lasagna noodles"

3 pounds ground beef, or combination of beef and pork

1 bunch fresh basil, diced (or 2 tablespoons dried)

1 teaspoon sea salt

2 cloves crushed garlic

2 cans diced tomatoes

3 cups crumbled goat cheese or dry curd cottage cheese (strict GAPS) or regular cottage cheese

2 cups mozzarella or cheddar cheese, shredded

1 cup grated parmesan cheese (optional)

Avocado oil to grease pans

--> Grill zucchini strips

--> Brown meat

--> Add diced basil, sea salt, and crushed garlic to browning meat

---> Add salt and pepper to cottage cheese

---> Layer lasagna ingredients in four 8x8 pans: Zucchini, diced tomatoes, browned meat, cottage cheese. Repeat, using zucchini slices on the top, and then top with mozzarella and optional parmesan. Cover with foil to freeze

Tip: This is a great meal to have tonight! Just pop one completed lasagna in the oven and bake covered for 30 minutes covered, 15 more minutes uncovered.

Tip: Extra zucchini? Add it to your roast veggies

Sausage-Stuffed Zucchini Boats

*Allergy Tip: ** This recipe is the dairy-free alternative to the zucchini lasagna – grocery list did not accommodate for both.*

5-6 pounds zucchini, sliced thinly lengthwise to make "lasagna noodles"

2 pounds ground beef mixture from meatballs

1 can diced tomatoes

1 bunch fresh basil, diced

2 tablespoons crushed garlic

Tip: Extra meat mixture? Either grill more zucchini boats, or store the meat mixture separately in the freezer. It is an excellent topping for Zoodles (zucchini noodles)

--> Using the rest of the veggies, combine vegetables and add to the oven to roast (can be frozen after roasting, or use within 5 days in the fridge)

Roasted Summer Vegetables

Don't stress if you don't have the exact amount of vegetables left over – we roast what we have left because this recipe is very forgiving, and delicious no matter what!

Tip: Once roasted, you can freeze these if needed. They also can be added to homemade stock as part of a soup - all the summer flavor, but perfect for a cool evening.

2 pounds summer squash

8 ounces button mushrooms

2 red onions, quartered

8 ounces cherry tomatoes

1/4 cup olive oil, avocado oil, or ghee

2 lemons, juiced

1 teaspoon fresh oregano

1 teaspoon sea salt

Freshly ground black pepper to taste

Combine all ingredients in a large bowl. Toss with large spoons or your hands, until vegetables are well coated. Transfer to oven-safe containers, whatever size you choose. Bake for 20 minutes. Cool, cover with foil, label, and freeze. Or continue baking another 20 minutes (total of 40) and keep in the fridge. Serve warm or cool, plain or drizzled with Italian dressing.

Need a break? Go ahead take one now if you need it.

Tip: If you're tired, go ahead and call it a day. Now the most important part of your cooking day is done!

Congratulations! You just prepared 15-18 entrees that are packed with protein and veggies! And you have your probiotic needs met as well, with quarts of pickled Italian veggies. And those sauces? They took only minutes to whip up since you had most of the ingredients out already, but you'll see over the coming week, they really bring a great addition of flavor AND nutrition to the meal! You rock!

Ready to keep going?

Let's make some zucchini muffins and a quick pudding that's simple to make since it's thickened with nutrient-dense gelatin.

Sweet: (Dairy-free!) Coconut Gelatin Pudding

2 (13.5-ounce) can full-fat coconut milk

6 egg yolks

1/2-1 cup honey

2 tablespoons pure vanilla

1 tablespoon gelatin

Ground cinnamon or sliced fruit, as garnish (optional)

Combine coconut milk, gelatin, egg yolks, honey, and vanilla in a medium-size saucepan with a fork. Allow gelatin to absorb liquid for 5 minutes.

Heat over medium heat until warm and a liquid, about 10 minutes.

Pour into individual glass bowls or a glass baking dish. Cover tightly then refrigerate for at least one hour or overnight. To serve, garnish as desired with fresh berries or cinnamon.

Grain Free Zucchini Muffins

Rich in protein from the almond flour and eggs, and a great way to use bountiful summer squash, these muffins are great for breakfast or alongside dinner.

Low Carb Tip: Omit the honey if looking for low carb options, these are delicious savory as well.

4 cups almond flour

10 eggs

4 cups shredded zucchini

1-1/2 teaspoon sea salt

1/4 cup honey

4 tablespoons coconut oil, ghee, or tallow to great muffin pan if needed

Shred zucchini with the grater attachment to the food processor. Mix all ingredients. Pour batter into 24 lined or well-greased muffin tins.

Bake at 350* for 20-30 minutes, or until a knife inserted comes out clean.

That's it! Look at everything we made! Congratulations, you're on your way to easy heat-and-serve meals for the next few weeks.

Mediterranean Meals - Storage and Reheating Instructions

Freezing & Reheating Instructions, and Menu Suggestions

Greek Shish Kebabs

To store: Use wire cutters to snip off the sharp ends and trim down skewers. Once trimmed, they will fit in a gallon zip-top bag.

Use within: 3-4 weeks.

Tips: If you want to keep them longer than 3-4 weeks, pre-cook at 350* for 15 minutes, this will stop the enzyme activity in the fresh vegetables and make them suitable for storing up to 6 months if kept in a freezer bag.

Reheat: From raw (not pre-cooked) thaw all day in the zip-top bag, placing the bag on a plate to catch drips if there are any leaks. In the evening, preheat oven to 350* and bake for 25-30 minutes on an oven-proof dish in a single layer.

Serving suggestions: Serve with coconut-dill dressing. Great for BBQs, potlucks (easy finger food!), and

Veggie-Packed Meatballs

To Store: Once cool, transfer to 1-2 gallon zip-top freezer bags. Place flat in the freezer. Flip bags once about 6 hours after placing them in the freezer to help the meatballs not to stick.

Use within: 6 months.

Reheat: Pan-fry in a tablespoon of fat over medium heat, drop into hot soup the last hour that it's in the crock pot, or cook, covered in hot soup on the stovetop over medium heat for 15 minutes.

Serving Suggestions: These are versatile! Serve with sauces, in soup, plain, in sandwiches, and more!

Greek Turkey Burgers

To Store: Allow to cool, place in 1-2 gallon zip-top bags. Freeze flat.

Use within: 6 months.

Reheat: Allow to thaw for at least 30 minutes. Heat in a dry skillet, or fry in a little fat over medium heat, 3-5 minutes on each side. Can be microwaved.

Serving Suggestions: Top with Coconut Dill Dressing, fresh onion rings, and serve in a lettuce wrap. Fresh fruit makes a delicious light side dish for this fresh meal.

Fermented Italian Vegetables

To Store: After initial fermentation, 'burp' your ferment (unscrew lid, and allow excess air to escape- do this over the sink) and then store in the fridge.

Use within: Once you start using a ferment, you introduce bacteria every time you open the jar, so try to use the jar within 10 days of first use. Otherwise, unopened (after the initial 'burping') ferments will stay in the fridge for 6 months or longer.

Reheat: Keep raw to keep enzymes and probiotics in tact.

Serving Suggestions: Serve alongside all meals as a condiment to provide needed probiotics. You may be surprised- children often LOVE ferments!

Dill Coconut Dressing

To Store: Keep covered, in the fridge.

Use within: 2 weeks.

Reheat: Not needed.

Serving Suggestions: Use on top of meat, vegetables, and as a flavorful topping for soup.

Italian Dressing

To Store: Keep covered, in the fridge.

Use within: 4 weeks

Reheat: Keep raw to preserve the health benefits of cold-pressed olive oil and raw vinegar.

Serving Suggestions: Use as salad dressing for fresh or steamed vegetables.

Zucchini Lasagna

To Store: Cover foil freezer container with foil. Once frozen, slip into a freezer zip-top bag or wrap with freezer paper.

Use within: 6 Months.

Reheat: Thaw. Bake at 350* for 45 minutes, covered for the first 30 minutes and then uncovered to finish melting the cheese for the last 15. Allow to rest 15 minutes before cutting.

Serving Suggestions: Serve with a fresh green salad, pickled italian vegetables, and zucchini muffins.

Stuffed Summer Squash

To Store: Cover foil freezer container with foil. Once frozen, slip into a freezer zip-top bag or wrap with freezer paper.

Use within: 6 months.

Reheat: Thaw. Bake covered at 350* for 25 minutes, or until heated through.

Serving Suggestions: Serve with a fresh green salad, pickled Italian vegetables, and zucchini muffins. Top zucchini boats with Italian Dressing.

Roasted Vegetables

To Store: Transfer cooled vegetables into a gallon zip-top bag, or quart bags if you want smaller serving sizes. Freeze fla.

Use within: 6 months.

Reheat: Bake in an oven-proof container after thawing for 30 minutes, or until heated through. Or heat on stovetop in a skillet over medium heat, covered, for 20 minutes.

Serving Suggestions: Can be added to 1 quart chicken stock and pureed with an immersion blender for a flavorful summer soup. Serve alongside meat warm or cold or tossed with fresh greens cold.

Coconut Pudding

To Store: Keep covered with plastic wrap in the fridge.

Use within: 10 days.

Reheat: Not needed.

Serving Suggestions: Garnish with fresh fruit.

Almond Flour Zucchini Muffins

To Store: Store in 2-3 gallon zip-top bags. Do not pack the bags too full, and do not squash in the freezer.

Use within: 3 months if frozen,

Reheat: Thaw. Eat cold, or toast in the toaster oven.

Serving Suggestions: Serve with honey for breakfast, or alongside dinner or lunch. These are protein-rich and have a generous amount of vegetables as far as muffins go!

Packed Lunches & Grab-and-Go Breakfasts

These lunches are suitable for freezing in case you want to make a couple week's worth at once. They are also designed to look like other children's packed lunches, to help children who may be self-conscious about eating differently fit in. Because of this, they contain more allergens (eggs, dairy, nuts) than other units in this book.

Recipe	Breakfast	Lunch
Yogurt	Homemade 'go-gurt'	Smoothie/Yogurt
Coconut Flour Waffles	Toasted for Breakfast	Used as Sandwich 'bread' for lunches
OJ Gummies		Treat
Breakfast Cookies	'in-a-pinch' Breakfast	Treat/Snack
Chia Jam	Pancake or Waffle Topping	Filing for sandwiches, topping for yogurt
Dried Fruit and Veggies		Snack
Pickled Carrots		Probiotic/Veggie

24-hour SCD Yogurt

Dairy free? Omit this recipe. It's just used for quick breakfasts- nothing else in this unit requires it. For those who eat dairy, this is a creamy treat on it's own, drizzled with honey, or sprinkled with raisins and flaked coconut! When you incubate it in individual 4-ounce cups, it's ready to serve in seconds!

Ingredients:

1/2 gallon whole milk

1 pint half and half or heavy cream

Yogurt starter (The Specific Carbohydrate Diet requires a yogurt starter with only acidophilus. On the GAPS diet plain high quality yogurt from the health food store can be used as the starter. See Grocery List for recommendations.)

Directions:

- In a stock pot, heat milk gently on medium heat, stirring approximately every 10 minutes, until milk is close to a boil.
- Cover, remove from burner, and allow to cool until the yogurt is comfortable to the touch, 90-110 degrees Fahrenheit.
- Make sure the yogurt is not too hot at this stage, or you will kill the good bacteria that are going to make your milk into yogurt.
- Pour nearly warm milk into clean quart jars.
- Using one tablespoon of commercial yogurt per quart, (or follow the directions that came with your powdered starter) mix yogurt or starter into the jars of warm milk.
- Cover and shake to distribute culture.
- Keep warm in a yogurt maker, Excalibur dehydrator or cooler at 100 degrees for a full 24 hours. Yogurt is now done and should be kept in the refrigerator.

Coconut Flour Waffles

These stay together in packed lunches so much better than sliced coconut flour bread. Due to all the eggs, they are protein rich and will keep the lunch-eater going all day long. The little pockets are perfect for holding chia jam or any other fillings of choice!

Ingredients:

4 Tablespoons melted coconut oil, butter, or ghee

1/2 cup coconut flour

12 eggs

2 Tablespoons vanilla extract, legal (watch for added sugar)

2 Tablespoons honey or 4 dates

1 apple, pureed or 1 cup pumpkin puree

1/2 tsp salt

Directions:

- Preheat waffle iron, grease generously with coconut oil.
- Mix all ingredients, and use a tablespoon to evenly distribute the batter on the iron and cook 3-4 minutes, or until golden brown.

OJ Gummies

Vibrant orange juice and the gut-healing power of gelatin. These look like typical fruit snacks or gummie bears, nobody else needs to know they're actually super health-giving!

Ingredients:

3 cups orange juice

2-4 tablespoons raw honey

1 cup gelatin

Directions:

- Combine all ingredients except gelatin. Add gelatin and use a whisk or

immersion blender to thoroughly combine juice and gelatin.
- Allow gelatin to absorb liquid for 5 minutes.
- Then heat over medium heat until gelatin all melts.
- Pour mixture into silicone candy molds or an 8×8-inch glass baking dish.
- Cover tightly and chill.

Chia Seed Jam

1 pound berries (strawberries, blueberries, raspberries)

¼ cup honey

2 tablespoons chia seeds

1 tablespoon lemon juice

- In a blender or with an immersion blender, puree berries.
- Add in honey and chia seeds and mix.
- Place in a pint mason jar, and allow to sit in the fridge for 4 hours, or longer, as the chia seeds absorb the liquid. Use as regular jam, keeping in the fridge.

Fermented Carrots

These are perfect ferments to pack because they look just like regular carrot sticks. They're packed with probiotics and are easier to digest for some of our kids with digestion issues.

2-3 lbs carrots

1 tbs sea salt per quart

Filtered water

Starter culture (optional- liquid from a successful batch of ferments)

- Scrub carrots, removed ends and any blemished bits. Cut into slices.
- Add 1 tablespoon unrefined sea salt per quart of carrots, and a splash of starter culture. Then fill with filtered water to cover the carrots (shake if necessary to settle).
- Allow to culture on the counter for 5-7 days, carrots will remain bright

orange and will soften a little. Transfer to the fridge to store. These can be frozen after the initial fermentation, after putting them in a lunch box.

Breakfast Cookies

In a pinch, these are great for breakfast on the way out the door. The coconut has fiber, nutbutter has fat and protein, and the honey holds it all together while giving it a sweet taste that everyone will love.

1/2 cup honey

1-1/2 cup Nutbutter

1/2 teaspoon sea salt (if unsalted)

1-1/2 cups flaked coconut (more if needed)

- Over medium-high heat, heat the honey to boil, and continue cooking, stirring occasionally over medium heat, for 3-5 minutes. Honey will be bubbling and starting to darken, but not be completely dark brown at this point.
- Turn off burner and add the peanutbutter and sea salt. Allow to sit for 5 minutes, or until the peanutbutter becomes more melty and stirs easily into the honey.
- Add in coconut while stirring. Add in more coconut if needed to make the mixture the consistency of cookie dough.
- Lay out parchment and, using a heaping tablespoon of the mixture, form into cookie shapes. Allow to cool to room temperature, and then store covered in the fridge.

Lunch Assembly & Finishing Up

- Depending on whether you are packing half a sandwich or a whole sandwich, make 10 or 5 sandwiches with the chia jam and coconut flour waffles. Cut into quarters and place in lunch container.

- Gummies should be set now, pop them out and add to lunches as desired.
- Add nutbutter/coconut cookies to lunches as desired.
- These can all freeze- freeze lunches now and add fresh sliced fruit and/or cultured carrots the morning before use.

- You may need to wait a while, but soon yogurt will be cool enough to touch. Do not try to incubate it if it is still too hot to hold your finger in comfortably for 10 seconds. If ready, add 1/2 teaspoon starter yogurt to each cup, fill with warm milk/cream, and cover with a lid. Lid does not need to be air or water tight. Incubate at 100-110*F for 24 hours. Transfer to fridge.
- If you did not use gummie molds for all your OJ Gummies, the 'block' gummies that were poured into a bowl or small container will take a few hours to set up. Once they set up, pop the whole block out onto a cutting board and then cut into small cubes with a large sharp knife. Once cubed, these can be stored in the freezer if desired.
- Allow carrots to culture for 5-7 days at room temp, and then 'burp' (allow air to escape), place lid back on, and move to the fridge.

Using Your Own Recipes

The great thing about meal prep is that you can adjust what works for you. Start as simple as browning 3 times as much ground beef as you need the next time you make taco salad, or as elaborate as turning two weeks' worth of groceries into 15 meals to be used throughout the month.

The tips below will help make your first bulk cooking experience on your own rewarding, or help you fine-tune what you've been doing for years with a few shortcuts. Either way, you'll reap the benefits of having delicious and healthy meals already prepared and waiting for you with minimal time investment.

Vary The Flavors in Your Meals

You may love Mexican food (who doesn't?!) but you're not going to want to eat taco salad 12 times this month. If you find yourself gravitating to the same spices (garlic, garlic, and more garlic anyone?) deliberately choose different flavor combinations like pineapple-sweetened pulled pork, ginger and garlic butternut squash soup, and curried beef with health-boosting turmeric and black pepper

Manage Your Time Realistically

What other obligations do you have while you're cooking? Do you have young children that you'll also be attending to? Older kids who are going to want to help (tips on this below)? A business that you're going to take calls for during your cooking time? Or do you have the whole day to devote to finding recipes, grocery shopping, cooking, storing, and clean up?

No matter what your situation, bulk cooking is fast paced, and a lot of work, so you may tire more quickly than you expected.

Prioritize Your Recipes

Prioritize cooking vegetables that will go bad in the fridge, and meat (like chicken) that you need for other things such as chicken stock or cooked chicken for chicken salad..

Choose protein and vegetables since they are most nutrient dense, yet the least exciting to prepare for. If you look at anyone's Pinterest page, you'll usually see a bunch of pins for sweets and desserts, and not so many for meat and vegetables. We're wired to be more excited about sugar than we are protein, so that's why it's essential to make our protein and vegetable dishes as easy as possible for the future. If all we have to do is thaw something and toss it in the oven or crockpot, it's suddenly super easy – and our health will thank us for it!

Last, do the fun baked goods like muffins or scones. You want to be able to bail on your last few recipes in case life gets in the way.

The one thing you do NOT want to bail on is kitchen clean up – so if you're in doubt, stop early and clean up!

Use Recipes That You Already Know You Like

Second only to waking up the next morning to every dish in your kitchen dirty because you didn't allow enough time and energy to clean up, the most disappointing thing that can happen with bulk cooking is that you end up with a bunch of food that you don't like the flavor or consistency of.

Tripling your family's favorite recipes, or quartering recipes designed for bulk cooking to test them in small batches, is always recommended over trying new things in huge quantities.

Personally we love coconut flour waffles, and I love making a ton of those for my freezer, but some people don't love them, especially if they're used to wheat-based waffles.

Always always always try the recipes ahead of time!

Printables

Get the free printable grocery lists, reheating instructions, and freezer bag labels that go along with this book by going to:

healthhomeandhappiness.com/freezer-cooking-club-printables

Want more instruction? Join the class with videos, bonus cooking units, and more!

www.freezercookingclass.com

Made in the USA
Las Vegas, NV
14 June 2022

50239801R00079